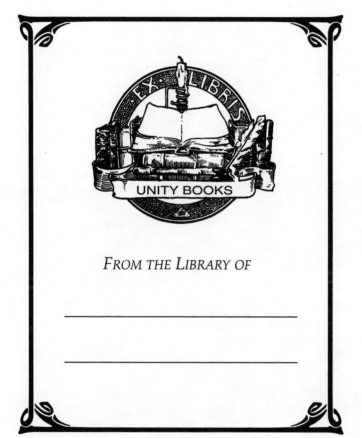

UNITY BOOKS

FROM THE LIBRARY OF

_____

_____

YOUR HOPE OF GLORY

Also by Elizabeth Sand Turner

Be Ye Transformed
Let There Be Light

YOUR HOPE OF GLORY

THE GOSPELS METAPHYSICALLY INTERPRETED

ELIZABETH SAND TURNER

Unity Classic Library

UNITY® Books

Unity Village, Missouri

Your Hope of Glory is a member of the
Unity Classic Library.

To receive a catalog of all Unity publications (books, cassettes,
and magazines) or to place an order, call the Customer Service
Department: (816) 251-3580 or 1-800-669-0282. For information, address Unity Books, Publishers, Unity School of
Christianity, 1901 NW Blue Parkway, Unity Village, MO
64065-0001.

First printing 1959; tenth printing 1996

Marbled design by Mimi Schleicher © 1994
Cover design by Jill L. Ziegler

Library of Congress Catalog Card Number: 90-070728
ISBN 0-87159-187-1
Canada GST R132529033

"We are confused when we first receive spiritual inspiration. . . . In the initial stage of our spiritual awakening, we are not aware of what is happening. It is different from any experience we have ever had. If we will be still, reassurance will come . . . we are to be receptacles for the outpouring of Spirit; we are to bring good into visible form."

Elizabeth Sand Turner

Lovingly Dedicated to
CHARLES FILLMORE
who helped untold numbers to find
in the Master's teachings "the food
which abideth unto eternal life."

PUBLISHER'S NOTE

The sources of quotations used in this book are indicated by the following initials:

ASP *Atom-Smashing Power of Mind*, Charles Fillmore
CE *Christ Enthroned in Man*, Cora Dedrick Fillmore
JC *Jesus Christ Heals*, Charles Fillmore
KL *Keep a True Lent*, Charles Fillmore
LT *Lessons in Truth*, H. Emilie Cady
MD *Metaphysical Bible Dictionary*, Charles Fillmore
MJ *Mysteries of John*, Charles Fillmore
TM *The Twelve Powers of Man*, Charles Fillmore
TT *Talks on Truth*, Charles Fillmore

Bible references are given in the usual way: (Mt. 1:1). Except in quoted material, or as otherwise noted, Bible quotations are from the Revised Standard Version.

CONTENTS

FOREWORD

What is the secret of Jesus' enduring influence? One basic reason is that humans are spiritual beings, made in the image and likeness of God. Everyone may not be aware of this, but we instinctively respond to the One whose every word and act was evidence of His divinity. The voice of our divine self may be faint; we may even deliberately close our ears to it, yet it continues to sound and ever urges a climb to higher ground. Jesus made this ascent, and by our spiritual kinship with Him we are drawn to Him. Charles Fillmore says:

"We are all in mind related to a great creative Spirit that infuses its very life into our minds and bodies when we turn our attention to it. We have mentally wandered away from this creative Spirit or Father-Mind and lost contact with its life-giving currents. Jesus made connection for us, and through Him we again begin to draw vitality from the great fountainhead" (JC 4).

For hundreds of years Hebrew seers had believed that a man was to come who would fulfill the noblest ideals of humanity. This ideal man, they foretold, would be the Messiah, the anointed One, the beloved of God, the Savior. They prophesied that He would lead His people out of darkness and distress into light and joy. From the days of Moses, who declared, ''The Lord your God will raise up for you a prophet like me from among you, from your brethren—him you shall heed'' (Deut. 18:15), throughout the period of the great literary prophets, there had been these predictions. How and when this Messiah was to come, the prophets did not know; nevertheless, they had a definite conception of what He would be like. Of all the prophets, Isaiah had the clearest vision. He said that a maiden would bear a son whose name would be Immanuel (which means God with us). He would be a redeemer, a king to whose sovereignty there would be no end:

''The people who walked in darkness have seen a great light; those who dwelt in a land of deep darkness, on them has light shined. . . . For to us a child is born, to us a son is given; and the government will be upon his shoulder, and his name will be called 'Wonderful Counselor, Mighty God, Everlasting Father, Prince of Peace' '' (Is. 9:2, 6).

Isaiah gave a lucid description of the nature of the anointed One:

"The Spirit of the Lord shall rest upon him, the spirit of wisdom and understanding, the spirit of counsel and might, the spirit of knowledge and the fear of the Lord. . . . He shall not judge by what his eyes see, or decide by what his ears hear; but with righteousness he shall judge the poor, and decide with equity for the meek of the earth; and he shall smite the earth with the rod of his mouth, and with the breath of his lips he shall slay the wicked. Righteousness shall be the girdle of his waist, and faithfulness the girdle of his loins" (Is. 11:2-5).

The prophet declared that the kingdom of the Messiah would be universal, not only for humanity but for all creation:

"The wolf shall dwell with the lamb, and the leopard shall lie down with the kid, and the calf and the lion and the fatling together, and a little child shall lead them. . . . They shall not hurt or destroy in all my holy mountain; for the earth shall be full of the knowledge of the Lord as the waters cover the sea" (Is. 11:6, 9).

Finally there came into the world the One who was to fulfill these great prophecies to the utmost—Jesus of Nazareth, who is Christ the Savior. Christ, from the Greek word *christos*, has the same meaning as the Hebrew word for Messiah.

According to the Unity teachings, the name *Jesus Christ* has a twofold meaning that should be clearly understood before you read farther. Jesus was the man of Galilee. Christ is the perfect spiritual self of everyone. Charles Fillmore states:

"Jesus represents God's idea of man in expression; Christ is that idea in the absolute. Jesus Christ was the type man, which includes all the mental phases through which man passes in demonstrating life's problems. So we find Jesus Christ passing through all the trials, temptations, and mental variations of each of us, 'yet without sin,' that is, not falling under the dominion of evil thoughts" (MD 345).

Unity believes that in The Gospels a spiritual meaning underlies characters and events. Jesus represents the spiritual person in activity. He is the outpicturing of the potential spiritual self that abides in each of us. His life therefore typifies stages in our own unfoldment. The Apostles represent the twelve spiritual faculties or powers that are to be brought forth in our lives. The Pharisees and Sadducees stand for qualities in the human consciousness that oppose or resist the Christ and should be eliminated.

Our real nature is like that of Jesus, for did He not say, "You are the light of the world" (Mt. 5:14), and bid us to let our light shine? He also said, "He who believes in me will also do the works that I do; and greater works than these will he do" (Jn. 14:12). We have indeed borne "the image of the man of dust" (1 Cor. 15:49); that is, through ignorance of our divine self we have functioned on a lower or earthly plane of consciousness; but, as Paul foresaw, "we shall also bear the image of the man of heaven" (1 Cor. 15:49). This higher state of consciousness is possible to all who follow Jesus and claim their divine heritage. His promise is, "I go to prepare a place for you. . . . That where I am you may be also" (Jn. 14:2-3). Through His great overcoming Jesus released the Christ consciousness into the universal ethers, and those who keep His word may enter into it. Jesus, therefore, is our Way-Shower and only Savior. Very often when we think of our Savior, we recall the words that

Charles Fillmore proclaimed to be the greatest words ever spoken: "Christ in you, the hope of glory" (Col. 1:27).

The material contained in this book covers the life and teachings of Jesus as interpreted by Unity School of Christianity and is based on the chronological sequence given in *A Harmony of the Gospels*, by A. T. Robertson, published by Harper and Brothers, New York City.

The four Gospels, Matthew, Mark, Luke, and John, are biographies of Jesus. Each presents a portrait of this Man among men. Mark's gospel, the first to be recorded, was written between A.D. 65 and 75 and is the shortest of the four. Apparently, little thought was given to the arrangement of material; yet, the writing is simple, clear, and vivid. The author, John Mark, accompanied Peter during the latter's missionary work in Rome, and he wrote of Jesus as Peter described Him. Through his words one pictures Jesus as the divine worker rather than as the Teacher, and feels the energy and intense activity with which Jesus performed His ministry.

The gospel of Matthew was written in the decade between A.D. 80 and 90, and endeavored to prove that Jesus was the Messiah of Jewish prophecy as well as the King of all peoples. Matthew's gospel is the longest of the four and contains practically all information that is found in Mark's gospel. Because of its effective grouping of the teachings of Jesus, notably those contained in the Sermon on the Mount, this Gospel precedes the other three in the Christian canon.

Luke's gospel was written only a few years after the gospel of Matthew. The writing incorporates much of Mark's gospel, but it has more continuity than the earlier two and is considered superior from a literary standpoint. Luke, a physician by profession, was a convert of Paul's and became his companion on missionary journeys. His writing reveals Jesus to the Gentile world as the Great Physician who healed souls and bodies.

The last of The Gospels was written by John toward the end of the first century A.D. Evidently he was acquainted with the three former gospels, and though he relates the major events as given in the Synoptic Gospels, Matthew, Mark, and Luke, he records many not known to them. His account begins not with the human Jesus, but with the divine Word, the same that was "in the beginning with God." He recounts fewer miracles and parables, but dwells more on the teaching of Jesus in the great Discourses, constantly picturing Jesus as the Son of God come to earth. His gospel touches profound depths of spirituality, rounding out and adding to the portrait of Jesus as given by Matthew, Mark, and Luke.

Each of the four writers tells of Jesus' wondrous deeds of mercy, His love for the Father and His fellowmen, His miracles, and finally of His crucifixion. Each tells of the glory of Easter morn and of His appearances after the Resurrection. Each emphasizes His greatness and also His nearness to those who believe.

Jesus is the most sublime character the world has known. He continues to hold a paramount place in all our lives, and hence in the affairs of the world. Those who accept Him and trust Him find a new and finer side of themselves coming into expression, a side they did not know they possessed. They discover that peace of mind is not something to be wished for, but something that is attained. They feel a love that makes God a reality and enables them to see Him in others. They detect in themselves a capacity to accomplish far beyond their former expectations. Not only individuals but countries that profess Christianity rise or fall in proportion to their ability to live according to the teachings of the Master. By understanding His life and following His teachings we may find salvation from all mortal limitation and do our part to bring the kingdom of All-Good to earth.

As we learn to take the steps in consciousness that Jesus taught, we discover that we are walking a better way, learning Truth, living happier and more useful lives. We are accepting the challenge proffered by Paul, "be renewed in the spirit of your minds." And imperceptibly, perhaps, yet very surely, we are actually putting on the "new nature, created after the likeness of God in true righteousness and holiness" (Eph. 4:24).

As you read the Master's majestic and inspiring words, may you feel His love poured out upon you and His power quickening your whole being. Then you, too, shall say with the Roman centurion and others who watched at the Cross, "Truly this was the Son of God!" (Mt. 27:54) Even as you make this acknowledgment, there shall come quickly to you His reassuring promise, "Lo, I am with you always, to the close of the age" (Mt. 28:20).

—Elizabeth Sand Turner

CHAPTER I

The Savior Is Born

"And in that region there were shepherds out in the field, keeping watch over their flock by night. And an angel of the Lord appeared to them, and the glory of the Lord shone around them, and they were filled with fear. And the angel said to them, 'Be not afraid; for behold, I bring you good news of a great joy which will come to all the people; for to you is born this day in the city of David a Savior, who is Christ the Lord. And this will be a sign for you: you will find a babe wrapped in swaddling cloths and lying in a manger.' And suddenly there was with the angel a multitude of the heavenly host praising God and saying, 'Glory to God in the highest, and on earth peace among men with whom he is well pleased!' "

—Luke 2:8-14

In these immortal words the Bible records the most momentous event in human history—the birth of Jesus. In 4 B.C. or near that time, there lived in the village of Nazareth of Galilee a Jew whose name was Joseph. He was a carpenter by trade, but the blood of Israel's kings flowed in his veins, for Joseph could trace his lineage back to David, the greatest of the Hebrew monarchs. Joseph was a kindly man and deeply religious. His family had originated in Bethlehem, but for some years Joseph had lived in Nazareth, where he became betrothed to Mary, a young Jewess of royal descent, and even more pious than Joseph. Tradition claims that Joseph was a widower and many years Mary's senior.

The New Testament gives very little information regarding Mary, but the Apocryphal Gospels are full of stories connected with her. These stories state that she was born to aged and childless parents, Joachim and Anna; that at the age of three she was dedicated to God at the Temple, and remained there until she was twelve, so increasing in virtue that angels ministered unto her; that as a young maiden she was betrothed to Joseph, who had been selected for her by a miraculous sign.

There are two accounts in The Gospels relating events immediately preceding the marriage of Joseph and Mary. Luke records the annunciation to Mary:

"In the sixth month the angel Gabriel was

sent from God to a city of Galilee named Nazareth, to a virgin betrothed to a man whose name was Joseph, of the house of David; and the virgin's name was Mary. And he came to her and said, 'Hail, O favored one, the Lord is with you!' But she was greatly troubled at the saying, and considered in her mind what sort of greeting this might be. And the angel said to her, 'Do not be afraid, Mary, for you have found favor with God. And behold, you will conceive in your womb, and bear a son, and you shall call his name Jesus. He will be great, and will be called the Son of the Most High; and the Lord God will give to him the throne of his father David, and he will reign over the house of Jacob for ever; and of his kingdom there will be no end.' And Mary said to the angel, 'How shall this be, since I have no husband?' And the angel said to her, 'The Holy Spirit will come upon you, and the power of the Most High will overshadow you; therefore the child to be born will be called holy, the Son of God' '' (Lk. 1:26-35).

Mary represents ''the soul that magnifies the Lord 'daily in the temple' and through its devotions prepares itself for the higher life'' (MD 427).

Because writers on spiritual subjects are not in complete agreement on their definition of the word *soul*, it is well to explain Unity's teaching as regards the threefold nature of humanity as Spirit, soul, and body:

"Spirit is I AM, the same in character as Divine Mind or God. Soul is man's consciousness—that which he has apprehended or developed out of Spirit; also the impressions that he has received from the outer world. Soul is both conscious and subconscious. Body is the form of expression of both spirit and soul" (MD 628).

In the Unity teachings the word *soul* is generally used to designate the total consciousness, but in Bible interpretation as given by Charles Fillmore, men represent that phase of the soul we term mind, and women represent the emotional or feeling nature of the soul.

Mary symbolizes the purified soul that has become highly intuitive and sensitive to inspiration from the Lord. To the soul in this state, an angel (spiritual thought) comes: "Hail, O favored one, the Lord is with you!"

We are confused when we first receive spiritual inspiration. (Mary was "troubled at the saying, and considered in her mind what sort of greeting this might be.'') In the initial stage of our spiritual awakening, we are not aware of what is happening. It is different from any experience we have ever had. If we will be still, reassurance will come: ''Do not be afraid, Mary, for you have found favor with God. And behold, you will . . . bear a son . . . . He will be great, and will be called the Son of the Most High,'' that is, we are to be receptacles for the outpouring of Spirit; we are to bring good into visible form. But how can this be? It is not in accord with the human laws with which we are familiar.

''And the angel said to her, 'The Holy Spirit will come upon you, and the power of the Most High will overshadow you; therefore the child to be born will be called holy, the Son of God' '' (Lk. 1:35).

Mary had become purified by spiritual aspiration and dedicated to the will of God. She was highly intuitive and thus receptive to a revelation from the Holy Spirit, and was aware of the quickening of new life. The idea of perfect humanity (Christ) was immaculately or spiritually conceived by her. This idea, filled with the life and wisdom of Spirit, was gradually to form its outer vehicle of expression, Jesus.

When a person's soul attains the degree of spiritual unfoldment represented by Mary, the "power of the Most High" overshadows it and there is conceived in the consciousness the idea of the indwelling Christ. This is "the child to be born" not of the human but of the divine, and "will be called holy, the Son of God." One's whole being is animated and vitalized by the outpouring of life from on high. Even as any idea that is dominant in consciousness comes into manifestation in time, so does this greatest of all ideas find embodiment in the changed lives of individuals. Their words and deeds express the Christ as did those of Jesus. Thus, the circumstances of Jesus' conception and virgin birth have great meaning for those who aspire to spiritual attainment.

"Unity accepts the virgin birth of Jesus, and finds in it a deep metaphysical significance. Though the virgin birth is considered a miraculous event, the Truth student should remember that the way of spiritual law transcends material law. 'The things which are impossible with men are possible with God.'

"Tradition tells us that Mary was not only virgin by reason of her unmarried state, but she was also virgin in mind and heart. We believe this has a symbolic meaning. Just as Jesus was born to one whose mind and heart were pure and uncorrupted, so too is the Spirit of Christ born into individual consciousness as the mind and heart are made pure and clean, freed of all mortal thought and sin.

"No one should feel that the manner of Jesus' birth made Him so different from the rest of mankind that we all cannot be perfect as He was perfect. It was Jesus' divine origin that gave Him power, not the peculiar circumstances surrounding His physical birth. Each individual, though he may be unaware of it, is a divine child of God, heir to all of God's goodness. Each bears the same relationship to God as Jesus: all are equally sons and children of the Most High" (pamphlet—"The New Birth," no longer available).

In the process of bringing a spiritual realization into manifestation, there is involved yet another faculty of the mind. Joseph, betrothed to Mary, represents understanding. We receive the idea of the indwelling Christ when the soul

(Mary) becomes sensitized to Spirit; but this revelation must be protected and sustained by understanding (Joseph). Even as Mary was at first troubled by the angel's announcement that she would bear a son, so, too, was Joseph. ''And her husband Joseph, being a just man and unwilling to put her to shame, resolved to divorce her quietly'' (Mt. 1:19). His intention to divorce Mary ''means that we do not in the first stages of the birth of Christ in us understand the process, and sometimes are moved to put it away from us'' (MD 367).

But when Joseph thought on these things, ''behold, an angel of the Lord appeared to him in a dream, saying, 'Joseph, son of David, do not fear to take Mary your wife, for that which is conceived in her is of the Holy Spirit; she will bear a son, and you shall call his name Jesus, for he will save his people from their sins' '' (Mt. 1:20-21).

Mary received a revelation from the Lord when the angel appeared to her, but Joseph received his revelation indirectly—the angel appeared to him in a dream. This signifies that spiritual enlightenment comes more directly through intuition than through understanding. However, when the understanding is illumined, it is obedient to divine guidance. Joseph acted on the inspiration he received, and devotedly cared for Mary.

Mary was aware of the divine life she carried. Desiring some time for quiet and meditation she went to the hill country to visit her cousin Elizabeth. Her devout and exalted frame of mind are expressed in the beautiful prayer of praise that has come to be known as the Magnificat:

> "My soul magnifies the Lord,
> and my spirit rejoices in God my Savior . . .
> for he who is mighty has done great things for
>   me,
> and holy is his name."
>
> —Luke 1:46-49

Such a state of exaltation nurtures the divine idea that has been quickened in the consciousness. Mary believed "in the so-called miraculous as a possibility. Mary expected the birth of the Messiah, according to the promise of the Holy Spirit" (MD 428).

It is only when we have been awakened to a realization of the divine life (Christ) in us that we are ready to give attention to the steps that must be taken in consciousness in order to express outwardly that which has been conceived inwardly. In the life of Jesus these steps are shown by His teachings, His healings, and His final overcoming. Jesus is spiritual man made manifest. Through Him we discover the way of salvation. "He will save his people from their sins" (Mt. 1:21).

Paul admonishes us, "have this mind among yourselves, which is yours in Christ Jesus" (Phil. 2:5). We should study this mind in order to emulate it. Jesus is the pattern. He is the example for all who would come into spiritual consciousness and express the Christ or divine self.

As the account of the life of Jesus is continued, it should be with the understanding that we are witnessing the unfolding of our own consciousness Godward. The events of His life are different from those we encounter, but the underlying principle is the same. In perceiving this, we can read of these events not only as happening to one man nearly 2,000 years ago, but also as stages in our own spiritual progress.

Shortly before Jesus' birth a decree was sent out by the Roman government that each Jew should enroll for taxation in his native city. As Joseph was of the lineage of David, it was necessary for him to go to Bethlehem for enrollment. Not wishing to leave Mary alone in Nazareth, Joseph took her with him on the journey:

"And while they were there, the time came for her to be delivered. And she gave birth to her first-born son and wrapped him in swaddling cloths, and laid him in a manger, because there was no place for them in the inn" (Lk. 2:6-7).

Bethlehem means "house of bread" and signifies divine substance. Substance is the spiritual essence that underlies all manifest form. The soul (Mary), heavily charged with the divine idea, had to be unified with substance before there could be a manifestation. But "in the inn" there is no room for the divine idea to come forth. The inn symbolizes both the human, worldly habitat and interest that has no place for spiritual things. Mary was the channel or vehicle for the expression of the Christ; but the birth had to be brought about in simplicity and quietness. This simplicity and quietness is symbolized in the fact that Jesus' birth took place in a cave or grotto where animals were kept.

The shepherds, who were the first to pay homage to the infant Jesus, represent those who have faith in God. To such persons illumination comes as "an angel" with the glad tidings that Christ the Savior is born. When we are obedient to the revelation and put forth effort to "see this thing that has happened" (Lk. 2:15), we find that the Christ is no longer a hope, but a reality. We then praise God for His life, which is manifested in our midst every day.

The shepherds told Mary and Joseph all that had occurred, and Mary "kept all these things, pondering them in her heart" (Lk. 2:19). In the depths of our being, the expression of divine life is sacred and not to be discussed promiscuously. We meditate on it, guard it, and revere it.

On the eighth day after His birth Jesus was circumcised, according to the Jewish custom. The word *circumcision* means "cutting off," and to the Jews it symbolized a cutting off of the sins of the human personality, and the dedication of the child to God. In the life of Jesus this law was fulfilled early, even as He later voluntarily fulfilled the law in every respect. However, in His life an additional significance is given to circumcision, even as it is to baptism and the keeping of the Sabbath.

"Under the law of Jesus Christ, circumcision is

fulfilled in its spiritual meaning—the purification of the individual from the law of sin and death. One is circumcised in the true inner significance of the word only by being thoroughly purified in soul. Then the glory of the inner soul cleansing and purifying works out into the outer consciousness and the body and sets one free from all sensual, corruptible thoughts and activities'' (MD 152).

The Mosaic law required each Jewish mother to have a period of purification after the birth of a child, a period of forty days in the case of a male child. After this, in order to complete her purification the mother must offer a year-old lamb and a young pigeon or turtledove, though persons in poorer circumstances might substitute another pigeon or turtledove for the lamb (Lev. 12). In order to comply with this law and the further requirement of presenting their son to the Lord, Mary and Joseph took Jesus to the Temple in Jerusalem. There Simeon, an aged priest, and Anna, a prophetess, met them and recognized Jesus as the promised Messiah. Simeon had received a promise from the Lord that he should not die until he had beheld the Savior. After he took the Child in his arms and praised God,

Simeon said:

"Lord, now lettest thou thy servant depart in
          peace,
    according to thy word;
    for mine eyes have seen thy salvation
    which thou hast prepared in the presence of all
          peoples,
    a light for revelation to the Gentiles,
    and for glory to thy people Israel."

                                 —Luke 2:29-32

Simeon symbolizes "one who listens and
obeys. Hearing, in its higher aspect, refers to the
state of mind in the devout Christian that looks
for and expects spiritual guidance and instruction direct from God. It may be summed up in
the word 'receptivity.' This new consciousness of
the indwelling immortal life takes the place of
hope, expectancy, obedience" (MD 619).

The good news of the birth of the Savior had
also reached the Wise Men. They had seen a star
in the heavens, which to them meant that one
had been born who would be "King of the
Jews." Journeying to Jerusalem, they inquired of
Herod the Great where they might find the new
King.

The Wise Men from the East represent:

"The stored-up resources of the soul, which rise to the surface when its depths are stirred by a great spiritual revelation. They are the inner realms of consciousness that, like books of life, have kept the records of past lives and held them in reserve for the great day when the soul would receive the supreme ego, Jesus. These 'Wise Men' represent the wisdom that is carried within the soul from previous incarnations. The east represents the within, man's inner consciousness" (MD 677).

Now Herod, knowing of the prophecies that there would come a Messiah, was greatly disturbed by the Wise Men's inquiry. He had been appointed king of the Jews by the Roman emperor in 40 B.C., and was well aware of the hatred the Jews held for him, for he was a foreigner and a symbol of their subjection to Rome. Herod, in turn, despised his subjects and was oppressive and often cruel in his treatment of them. Realizing that his throne might be in jeopardy, he called together the chief priests and scribes, and asked where their scriptures predicted the Messiah would be born. Upon being

informed that Bethlehem was the place foretold, Herod sent the Wise Men there with instructions to return to him when they had found
the Child so that he, too, might worship Him.
However, his real intent was to have the Babe
slain.

"When they had heard the king they went
their way; and lo, the star which they had seen in
the East went before them, till it came to rest
over the place where the child was. When they
saw the star, they rejoiced exceedingly with great
joy; and going into the house they saw the child
with Mary his mother, and they fell down and
worshiped him. Then, opening their treasures,
they offered him gifts, gold and frankincense
and myrrh" (Mt. 2:9-11).

The gifts of the Magi represent "the inner resources of Spirit, which are open to the Christ
Mind. Gold represents the riches of Spirit;
frankincense, the beauty of Spirit; myrrh, the
eternity of Spirit" (MD 677).

Herod signifies "the ruling will of the
physical, the ego in the sense consciousness"
(MD 274). This will ever seeks to destroy that
which is spiritual, because it sees in the things of

Spirit a power that threatens its rule.

The Wise Men were warned in a dream not to return to Jerusalem, so they "departed to their own country by another way" (Mt. 2:12). Herod, failing to receive a report from the Wise Men, became exceedingly fearful. In an effort to make secure his throne, he issued an edict that all male children under two years of age, living in Bethlehem or the surrounding country, should be put to death. Herod, however, did not accomplish his purpose, for Joseph (understanding) was warned in a dream to flee into Egypt with Mary and Jesus.

Egypt typifies the sense place of thought that temporarily harbors the Christ. After Joseph spent a period of time there, he was divinely guided to leave and return to his native land. Herod the Great had died, and his son Archelaus reigned. When Joseph heard this, he did not go to Jerusalem, "and being warned in a dream he withdrew to the district of Galilee. And he went and dwelt in a city called Nazareth" (Mt. 2:22-23). The return to Nazareth was necessary, for Nazareth represents "the commonplace mind of man, but it is a place of development, through which the Christ comes into expression" (MD 473).

CHAPTER II

The Voice in the Wilderness

*"And the child grew and became strong,
filled with wisdom; and the favor of God
was upon him."*

—Luke 2:40

When Jesus had completed His twelfth year
He was allowed to accompany Mary and Joseph
from their home in Nazareth to the Holy City for
the observance of the great Feast of the Passover.
At this age a Jewish boy became a "son of the
Law," a status that implied spiritual responsibility, and we find Jesus attending His first
passover to discharge this responsibility.

We can imagine how strange and vastly interesting to the Nazarene lad was His first journey
to Jerusalem, a distance of approximately eighty
miles. As was the custom in those days, Jesus and
His parents joined a group of Galilean pilgrims
and, together, the band made its way slowly
south through Samaria to Judea, a journey of
four or five days.

The city of Jerusalem was teeming with visitors
from many parts of Palestine and from various

countries in the Mediterranean area, for Jewish pilgrims and proselytes came yearly to the Temple for celebration of the great feasts, of which there were several. Notable among them were the Passover, the Feast of Tabernacles, and the Feast of the Dedication. In this particular instance the crowds were drawn to the city on the occasion of the Feast of the Passover. This feast commemorated the deliverance of the Jews from Egyptian bondage under the leadership of Moses.

The observance of the Feast of the Passover lasted a week. When the ceremonials were over, the Galilean caravan started homeward. It is understandable that in such a large group a boy might easily be lost sight of, and Mary and Joseph did not notice Jesus' absence until they had gone a day's journey. We can imagine their dismay when their inquiries among kinsmen and acquaintances failed to disclose His whereabouts. Hastily they returned to Jerusalem to seek Him:

"After three days they found him in the temple, sitting among the teachers, listening to them and asking them questions; and all who heard him were amazed at his understanding and his answers. And when they saw him they

were astonished; and his mother said to him,
'Son, why have you treated us so? Behold, your
father and I have been looking for you anxious-
ly.' And he said to them, 'How is it that you
sought me? Did you not know that I must be in
my Father's house?' And they did not understand the saying which he spoke to them'' (Lk.
2:46-50).

This was Jesus' first announcement of His dedication to God's service. He had reached the age
of twelve, and this number spiritually interpreted signifies completeness or wholeness. We
have attained the first stage of spiritual maturity
when we understand and acknowledge that we
must be in our ''Father's house,'' or ''about my
Father's business,'' as the Authorized Version of
the Bible gives it. It should be our vital concern
to learn God's law, to express His qualities that
are latent within us, and to do His work.

''And he went down with them and came to
Nazareth, and was obedient to them; and his
mother kept all these things in her heart. And
Jesus increased in wisdom and in stature, and in
favor with God and man'' (Lk. 2:51-52).

All great leaders have periods of preparation for the work they are to do. This is especially true of those who set themselves to serve God. No doubt the eighteen years that followed Jesus' appearance in the Temple served as a time of inward preparation for Him.

All Jewish boys were taught a trade. Jesus learned carpentry from Joseph. Joseph is not mentioned after Jesus began His ministry, and it is assumed that he died before this time. Possibly, Jesus took Joseph's place as head of the family. In addition to His work, however, He must have spent many hours in study, meditation, and prayer. No one advances in "wisdom and stature" without using his time to advantage. There have been many speculations as to Jesus' activity during the so-called "silent years" of His life, but The Gospels, the only reliable record, indicate that He spent them uneventfully in the little village of Nazareth. Charles Fillmore says:

"Jesus was imbued with a spirit purely His own. He did not borrow His mission, or His words, or His precepts from Egypt, Persia, or India. He was a genius that burned with His own wick and oil" (TT 67).

At the age of thirty Jesus left Nazareth and journeyed to the place on the banks of the Jordan River in Judea where John the Baptist was preaching and baptizing.

John formed the connecting link between Judaism and Christianity by his recognition of Jesus as the Messiah long promised by Hebrew prophecy. His mission was to prepare the Jews for Jesus' message, and this he did with all the ardor of the reformer that he was.

"I am the voice of one crying in the wilderness, 'Make straight the way of the Lord' " (Jn. 1:23), cried this great forerunner of Jesus.

From the standpoint of spiritual interpretation John the Baptist plays an essential role. He represents the illumined intellect; that is, the mind turned toward spiritual things. The mind can function on various levels of consciousness. When a person is concerned exclusively with worldly considerations, his mentality expresses on the lowest or sense level. As he progresses mentally, the more intangible values of life command his attention. The faculties of reason and judgment develop and gradually supersede more instinctual desires. Moving still higher in mental development, he becomes aware of the existence of a spiritual realm and longs to know more of it.

In time spiritual concerns entirely outweigh material or purely intellectual ones, for a divine idea has illumined the mind. This is the John-the-Baptist consciousness. Charles Fillmore states:

"He [John] signifies a high intellectual perception of Truth, but one not yet quickened of Spirit. John represents that attitude of mind in which we are zealous for the rule of Spirit. This attitude is not spiritual, but a perception of spiritual possibilities and an activity in making conditions in which Spirit may rule" (MD 357).

In individual unfoldment, we begin our conscious identification with God in that mental state symbolized by John. And even as the prophet (John) was the forerunner of the Savior (Jesus), so, too, is the illumined intellect the predecessor of full spiritual realization. Thus, a study of John's life and ministry reveals steps on our spiritual way. Only as we understand and profit by the greatness and also the limitations of the intellect can we move forward toward the Christ consciousness.

John was the son of Zechariah, a priest, and Elizabeth, elderly Jews who lived in Judea. They had long wanted a son but it seemed that their prayers were not to be answered. Yet one day as Zechariah was performing his duties at the Temple in Jerusalem:

"There appeared to him an angel of the Lord standing on the right side of the altar of incense. And Zechariah was troubled when he saw him, and fear fell upon him. But the angel said to him, 'Do not be afraid, Zechariah, for your prayer is heard, and your wife Elizabeth will bear you a son, and you shall call his name John. And you will have joy and gladness, and many will rejoice at his birth; for he will be great before the Lord . . . and he will be filled with the Holy Spirit . . . . And he will turn many of the sons of Israel to the Lord their God, and he will go before him in the spirit and power of Elijah, to turn the hearts of the fathers to the children, and the disobedient to the wisdom of the just, to make ready for the Lord a people prepared' " (Lk. 1:11-17).

Metaphysically, Zechariah represents spiritual consciousness, and Elizabeth signifies the soul in the feminine or love consciousness (MD 684, 193). Together they represent the whole consciousness, thought and feeling, expressing on the spiritual plane. Hence, they were receptive to a divine idea (an angel of the Lord). Note, however, that just as we are often awed by the revelation of Spirit and find it difficult to accept, so, too, was Zechariah fearful and doubting. "How shall I know this? For I am an old man, and my wife is advanced in years" (Lk. 1:18). Because of his doubt Zechariah was struck dumb. The implication here is that disbelief keeps us from speaking the word that has been revealed. Zechariah was released from dumbness when John was born, and he praised and gave thanks to God:

"Blessed be the Lord God of Israel,
  for he has visited and redeemed his people."
  —Luke 1:68

Elizabeth, the mother of John, and Mary, the mother of Jesus, were cousins; hence, Jesus and John were related. This tells us that the intellect in its highest state is closely connected with spiritual realization, perceiving the Christ and striving to prepare the consciousness to accept the divine idea.

John was less than a year older than Jesus. Before he began his public work, he lived the life of

an ascetic in the Judean wilderness near the
shores of the Dead Sea. In his secluded haunt
John studied the words of God and gradually became convinced that the prophecies concerning
a Messiah were about to be fulfilled. The
Anointed One, the Messiah, was to usher in the
kingdom of heaven and redeem His people from
all bondage, but they must be prepared to receive and follow Him. Holiness was required of
them, and in this way they were sadly lacking.
Among the masses there was much corruption;
hypocrisy lurked in the ranks of the religious
leaders. The Baptist saw it as his duty to denounce such leaders in scathing words and to
proclaim the way of righteousness.

John was about thirty years old when he appeared on the banks of the Jordan and preached,
speaking with all the vigor and authority that
characterized the prophets of old. The Jews were
startled, yet drawn to him. There had been no
prophetic voice for several hundred years.
Though the early prophets had often been persecuted by their contemporaries, later generations
revered them. Now the throngs listened eagerly
to the words of one whom they recognized as a
man of God. From near and far they flocked to
the banks of the Jordan to hear him.

Even John's appearance was significant. He wore "a garment of camel's hair, and a leather girdle around his waist; and his food was locusts and wild honey" (Mt. 3:4). Such had been the costume of the earlier prophets, the camel's hair or sackcloth symbolizing repentance. The Mosaic law sanctioned the eating of locusts and wild honey.

The keynote of John's message was "Repent, for the kingdom of heaven is at hand" (Mt. 3:2). Every Jewish heart thrilled at the words *the kingdom of heaven is at hand*, for this meant to them that the Messiah was soon to come. That John prefaced this announcement with the command, "Repent," made little difference to the Jews until he made it quite clear that they were in dire need of reforming and could not enter the kingdom without doing so. The illumined intellect understands that a change must take place in the individual before the kingdom can become a reality. As descendants of Abraham the Jews claimed the right to enter the kingdom of heaven to be set up by the Messiah. They were not prepared for John's command for repentance. Neither did they like his analysis of the conditions brought on by their sins. But repentance is a necessary step in the attainment of righteousness, and of one and all John demanded:

"Bear fruits that befit repentance, and do not begin to say to yourselves, 'We have Abraham as our father'; for I tell you, God is able from these stones to raise up children to Abraham" (Lk. 3:8).

To repent means to change one's mind. In a spiritual sense repentance is the act of turning from materialism and reaching for spiritual things. We cannot build a spiritual consciousness until we are willing to rid the mind of the beliefs and habits of thought that belong to the lower nature. John warned that only those who were willing to reform could receive the blessing of the coming kingdom. The choice was at hand:

"Even now the axe is laid to the root of the trees; every tree therefore that does not bear good fruit is cut down and thrown into the fire" (Lk. 3:9).

In the Jordan, John baptized those who were willing to repent. Regarding this baptism, Charles Fillmore states:

"Water baptism symbolizes a cleansing process, the letting go of error. It is the first step in the realization of Truth. It is the process of pouring into consciousness the dissolving power of the Word, which breaks up and washes away all thoughts of materiality. . . . Water baptism indicates a letting-go attitude of thought, denial" (MD 96).

Unity teaches that water baptism represents the purification of the consciousness and that actually the symbol (water) is unnecessary. Denial is the mental process of cleansing false thoughts from the mind by repudiating them. We deny anything that is not true of Spirit even though it may seem to be true from an earthly point of view. An affirmation is a statement of Truth. We first make a denial of error, and then we affirm that which is good. Denials erase errors from the mind, and affirmations establish spiritual ideas. The water baptism of John represents denial. The spiritual baptism of Jesus that was predicted by John and given the Apostles after the Resurrection represents affirmation. (See Chapter XIV for spiritual baptism.)

John spoke of spiritual things with the voice of authority. This led many people to ask him if he

was the Christ, but John never failed to acknowledge the supremacy of Jesus. He said:

"I baptize you with water for repentance, but
he who is coming after me is mightier than I,
whose sandals I am not worthy to carry; he will
baptize you with the Holy Spirit and with fire"
(Mt. 3:11).

When Jesus came to John to be baptized John
said:

" 'I need to be baptized by you, and do you
come to me?' But Jesus answered him, 'Let it be
so now; for thus it is fitting for us to fulfil all
righteousness.' Then he consented. And when
Jesus was baptized, he went up immediately
from the water, and behold, the heavens were
opened and he saw the Spirit of God descending
like a dove, and alighting on him; and lo, a voice
from heaven, saying, 'This is my beloved Son,
with whom I am well pleased' " (Mt. 3:14-17).

From this time, the baptism of Jesus by John,
the lives of the two men were to touch on several
occasions until John was slain during the latter
part of the second year of Jesus' ministry. How-

ever, in order to conclude the teaching regarding the illumined intellect (John), the remaining events of the Baptist's life will follow in this chapter.

Shortly after the baptism John saw Jesus and said to his disciples, "This is the Son of God" (Jn. 1:34). Later, when Jesus began His ministry in Judea near the banks of the Jordan where John was preaching, some of his followers reported that Jesus was gaining more disciples than he was. The Baptist replied:

"No one can receive anything except what is given him from heaven. You yourselves bear me witness, that I said, I am not the Christ, but I have been sent before him. He who has the bride is the bridegroom; the friend of the bridegroom, who stands and hears him, rejoices greatly at the bridegroom's voice; therefore this joy of mine is now full. He must increase, but I must decrease" (Jn. 3:27-30).

The illumined intellect (John) has a fourfold task in preparing the consciousness to receive the Christ: it declares the kingdom at hand; it counsels repentance; it purifies the mind by means of denials (water baptism); and it points to a greater one who is to come (the Christ).

John's limitation lay in his belief in evil as a reality and in contending with it. He denounced the Pharisees who came to hear his message, calling them a "brood of vipers" (Mt. 3:7). He rebuked Herod Antipas, King of Galilee, for his marriage to Herodias, his brother Philip's wife. This marriage was in violation of the Mosaic law to be sure, but condemnation rarely corrects wrongdoing. Jesus admonished nonresistance to evil. The way of overcoming is through allying ourselves with God, not by fighting evil. We should learn to give good only. Did not Jesus say, "If any one strikes you on the right cheek, turn to him the other also" (Mt. 5:39)? If we have a staunch faith in the power of God to right a condition, He will instruct us how to handle outer things. Under His guidance evils can be corrected in a harmonious way and for the good of all concerned. In keeping our attention on Him we may look through evil and perceive the good (God) and thus aid in bringing it into manifestation.

Herod Antipas, stung by the reproof of John, wanted to have him slain, but he feared an uprising of the people for they loved the Baptist. Finally, goaded on by his wife Herodias, the king imprisoned him in a lonely fortress near the Dead Sea. Metaphysically, this means that the illumined intellect (John) is restricted by willful thoughts (Herod) and licentious emotions (Herodias).

"John the Baptist in prison represents the intellect hemmed in, imprisoned, because of its magnifying sin and evil and condemning them. Some persons see the evil in the world as a power so formidable that it paralyzes all their efforts, and they accomplish nothing in the service of Truth" (MD 358).

If we continue to acknowledge sin and struggle against it, we finally reach a point of uncertainty and doubt in consciousness. We are likely to lose faith when outer conditions are trying, even though it has formerly been revealed to us that Spirit is supreme and we have declared this. This is what happened to John. While in prison he began to doubt his own revelation that Jesus was the promised Messiah, and sent two of his disciples to Galilee to inquire of Jesus, "Are you he who is to come, or shall we look for another?" (Mt. 11:3) Perhaps Jesus had not done what John expected or desired. Sometimes we pray for and expect the outworking of a situation in a certain way and are disappointed when our expectations are not fulfilled. Then we wonder if our spiritual prompting was genuine. Do not be confused when moments of doubt come; ask as John did.

"Jesus answered them [John's disciples], 'Go and tell John what you hear and see: the blind receive their sight and the lame walk, lepers are cleansed and the deaf hear, and the dead are raised up, and the poor have good news preached to them' '' (Mt. 11:4-5).

Jesus did not need to say that He was the Messiah. His works bore witness of Him. He knew John would understand that only a divine power which moved through Him could enable Him to perform the miracles that had been accomplished. If in our moments of perplexity we will be still, we will receive confirmation from Christ that He is truly our all-sufficiency in everything. Each of us has felt the Christ presence. We have seen evidences of His healing power. Yet now and then we need the reassurance that He is with us and that His work is being done.

Jesus knew the greatness of John, but He also knew John's limitations. He said:

"Among those born of women there has risen no one greater than John the Baptist; yet he who is least in the kingdom of heaven is greater than he" (Mt. 11:11).

Jesus' words mean that those who depend on and use their spiritual qualities even to a small extent are nearer the kingdom (greater) than those who may be more enlightened along intellectual lines.

John met his death by order of Herod Antipas. The dramatic story is fully narrated in Mark 6:14-29. At a sumptuous feast given by Herod, Herodias' daughter (whose name was Salome, according to tradition) so pleased the king by her dance that he impulsively offered to grant any wish she might make, even to the half of his kingdom. "And she went out, and said to her mother, 'What shall I ask?' And she said, 'The head of John the baptizer' " (Mk. 6:24). Herod immediately regretted his rash promise but felt that he could not withdraw it before his guests. He commanded a soldier to go to John in prison and bring back the head of the valiant champion of righteousness. The higher thought (John) is thus temporarily overcome by the unregenerate emotions (Herodias), but its work of turning the mind toward God has been accomplished. Charles Fillmore states:

"The death of John the Baptist . . . refers to the passing away of that first enthusiasm for character reform which possesses the disciple at the earthly stage of his experience. This John-the-Baptist phase is not the permanent state of consciousness, but is to be followed by one that is permanent" (MD 358).

CHAPTER III

Jesus' Ministry Begins

In going to John the Baptist for baptism, Jesus sought to identify Himself with the good that John was doing in teaching the people to repent. In stating that He wished to "fulfill all righteousness," Jesus was seeking a contact with all that John represented. John was the last prophet of the old dispensation. There should be no separation between the two, but rather a merging from the old to the new. Here Jesus clearly indicated that His teaching was not to debase the highest ideals of Judaism, but was to expand their spiritual meanings.

Whenever there is a complete cleansing of the consciousness (water baptism), a spiritual illumination follows. As Jesus emerged from the river, the Holy Spirit descended on Him "like a dove" (symbol of gentleness, peace, and new-creating life), and a voice (clear realization) came, bringing the announcement of His true identity: "This is my beloved Son, with whom I am well pleased" (Mt. 3:17).

Immediately after His baptism Jesus "was led up by the Spirit into the wilderness to be

tempted by the devil'' (Mt. 4:1). The attainment of a higher consciousness is generally followed by a testing period to give us opportunity
to prove that we have accepted and can use the
illumination received. The individual consciousness must be disciplined and tested before it can
become master of the thoughts. In the development of the Christ mind, an entirely new and
wider set of ideas and situations has to be met.
Jesus' experiences in the wilderness are to show
us how to deal with the thoughts and desires of
the senses, and to place them under proper disci-
pline. It requires spiritual discernment and un-
selfish devotion to the highest Truth to meet and
overcome the temptations of the personal consciousness.

The Devil is the ''adverse consciousness that
has been built up in ignorance and disregard of
the divine law'' (MD 346). Jesus had taken on
the limitations of the flesh or senses and was,
therefore, tempted in all points even as we are.
He, too, had to meet the errors of the race
thought. ''And he fasted forty days and forty
nights, and afterward he was hungry'' (Mt. 4:2).

Charles Fillmore states:

''The forty days' fast is an all-round denial of

sense demands. In fasting, we in our thoughts live above the material needs. We are 'led up' and our appetites and passions are for a season in such an eclipse that we think that they will trouble us no more. But 'afterward he was hungry.' There is a return to sense consciousness'' (MD 346).

Three great temptations were presented to Jesus, and He met them within His own consciousness, even as we must do. They are typical of the enticements that come to us when we realize that we have access to spiritual power. How are we going to use this power? To benefit the personal, or for the glory of God? Jesus is our great Teacher, and His experience shows us how these temptations should be met.

The first temptation was:

'' 'If you are the Son of God, command these stones to become loaves of bread.' But he answered, 'It is written, ''Man shall not live by bread alone, but by every word that proceeds from the mouth of God'' ' '' (Mt. 4:3-4).

Is one ever justified in using spiritual power to gain material wealth, even if it is to be used for what one considers a worthy purpose? That God prospers those who trust and obey Him is attested throughout the Scriptures, but to center our whole attention on substance in the form of material supply defeats the purpose of a spiritual ministry. In addition:

"The temptation to turn stones into bread illustrates the thought of ignorance that deceives people with the belief that they can satisfy the soul with materiality, without looking for the bread that comes from heaven, the Word of God. We must feed our soul with new truths daily, that we may grow in spiritual ways" (MD 346).

The second temptation was:

"Then the devil took him to the holy city, and set him on the pinnacle of the temple, and said to him, 'If you are the Son of God, throw yourself down; for it is written, "He will give his angels charge of you" and "On their hands they will bear you up, lest you strike your foot against a stone." ' Jesus said to him, 'Again it is written, "You shall not tempt the Lord your God" ' " (Mt. 4:5-7).

This was a particularly subtle temptation, for there was a belief among the Jews that the Messiah was to appear in some spectacular manner. Had Jesus performed a feat of this sort, He would have called immediate attention to Himself. His desire was to serve humankind. Would He not be entitled to secure a following by performing a miracle? Charles Fillmore states that this temptation "means that no display of spiritual power for personal glory should be made. We cannot make a display of our spiritual power with safety" (MD 346). We should never speak the word of healing with the thought in mind to prove that Truth "works," or attempt to demonstrate any good for the purpose of convincing others that it can be done.

The third temptation was:

"Again, the devil took him to a very high mountain, and showed him all the kingdoms of the world and the glory of them; and he said to him, 'All these I will give you, if you will fall down and worship me.' Then Jesus said to him, 'Begone, Satan! for it is written, "You shall worship the Lord your God and him only shall you serve" ' " (Mt. 4:8-10).

We should never allow ourselves to be under
the dominion of the personal consciousness. It
promises power that it cannot give, and to yield
to its alluring voice would pave the way for our
own destruction:

"To worship the Devil is to worship personality; to live in personal consciousness and give it
the substance of our life and thought. When the
temptation arises in our consciousness to use our
God-attained spiritual faculties and powers for
the building of our personal ambitions, we
should know that under the divine law there is
but one worthy of our worship and service, the
Lord God. To serve God we must build up spirituality in mind, body, and affairs" (MD 346).

Jesus met each of the three types of temptation by speaking the word of Truth. The Christ
spirit will not permit God-power to be used for
selfish ends. Jesus quoted from Deuteronomy in
the Old Testament, thus showing His familiarity
with these writings. It is helpful to memorize
some of the favorite verses and promises that we
find in the Bible. These are really affirmations of
Truth, and by pondering them our minds become imbued with spiritual ideas. In an hour of

temptation these ideas come readily to mind. By our holding steadfastly to them the claims of the mortal are refuted. The strength of the Almighty moves through us, and we are able to rise above negative conditions.

"Then the devil left him, and behold, angels came and ministered to him" (Mt. 4:11).

When we realize our unity with God and know that we achieve development only through singleness of mind and heart, the Devil (personality) leaves us, and we are content to worship God only. Then "angels," which are our perceptive qualities quickened to the higher level of Spirit, minister to us. To gain self-understanding and self-dominion is the work of God that all of us must accomplish for ourselves.

When we surmount temptations, we experience release in mind and body, and feel the peace and comfort of Spirit. The overcoming of temptation is our own choosing. It is not the way of selfishness, even though it may seem to be a claiming of the good that is ours by divine right. It is the way of righteousness, and we have chosen it, since we love the Most High.

After the years of inner preparation in Naza-

reth, His baptism by John the Baptist, and His
temptation in the wilderness, Jesus was fully
equipped to show others the way to redemption.
He was ready to begin His public ministry, generally reckoned to have lasted about three years.
The number *three* represents the Trinity, or God
as threefold in Being—Father, Son, and Holy
Spirit. Symbolically, the trinity represents mind,
idea, and expression; or thinker, thought, and
action. We are likewise threefold as Spirit, soul,
and body. Thus, we can say that the years of
Jesus' ministry signify a completed activity.

We should approach this time of Jesus' life
with the clear understanding that He represents
the spiritual in expression. The spiritual self,
conceived and brought forth by the purified
soul, Mary, is now to render its great service
through the man, Jesus. In Jesus we see the ideal
functioning in all the common affairs of life with
the wisdom, love, and power of God. Since we
were created in the image and likeness of our
Creator, it is our right and privilege to follow the
great Way-Shower, first in consciousness and
then in deed.

The first year of Jesus' ministry may be called
"the year of obscurity," for during this time He
was slowly coming into prominence. The events

of this period are scanty. The overcoming of three temptations marked the end of Jesus' preparatory period. He then returned to the banks of the Jordan where John the Baptist was preaching. When the Baptist saw Him he said to the two disciples who were with him, "Behold, the Lamb of God!" (Jn. 1:36) One of these disciples was Andrew, and it is thought that John was the other. These two immediately left the Baptist and followed Jesus:

"Jesus turned, and saw them following, and said to them, 'What do you seek?' And they said to him, 'Rabbi . . . where are you staying?' He said to them, 'Come and see' " (Jn. 1:38-39).

When the illumined intellect (John the Baptist) reveals the presence of the spiritual (Jesus), we are greatly interested and ask, "Where are you staying?" Where is the habitat of the Christ? No one can tell us, not even Jesus as a man. He does, however, issue an invitation, "Come and see." We "come" by turning in mind and heart to the things of Spirit. We want the things of Spirit, yet we are often reluctant to release worldly interests. Our desires are for both spiritual and material blessings, but the latter can be secured permanently only if we seek first the kingdom of God and His righteousness. We must be willing to leave the outer and turn to the inner. How else can we know where He lives? To follow Him (''come'') is an inward, spiritual journey. If we take it, we shall discover (''see'') the abiding place of the Christ.

After Andrew had contacted Jesus, he lost no time in finding his brother Simon Peter to whom he exuberantly exclaimed, ''We have found the Messiah'' (Jn. 1:41). Immediately Simon Peter went also to Jesus, and when Jesus saw him He said, '' 'So you are Simon the son of John? You shall be called Cephas' (which means Peter)'' (Jn. 1:42). Jesus was quick to recognize the one who was to become His foremost apostle.

The next day, Jesus returned to Galilee and went to the city of Bethsaida. There He saw Philip, a fisherman, to whom He gave the invitation, ''Follow me'' (Jn. 1:43). Philip promptly sought his friend, Nathanael (called Bartholomew in the Synoptic Gospels, as this was probably Nathanael's surname), and announced, ''We have found him of whom Moses in the law and also the prophets wrote, Jesus of Nazareth, the son of Joseph'' (Jn. 1:45). Nathanael was somewhat skeptical, for Nazareth was an obscure, even an ill-reputed village, and in Nathanael's opinion it was no place for the home of the Messiah. "Can anything good come out of Nazareth?" he asked. Philip silenced him with the words, "Come and see" (Jn. 1:46).

"Jesus saw Nathanael coming to him, and said of him, 'Behold, an Israelite indeed, in whom is no guile!' Nathanael said to him, 'How do you know me?' Jesus answered him, 'Before Philip called you, when you were under the fig tree, I saw you.' Nathanael answered him, 'Rabbi, you are the Son of God! You are the King of Israel!' Jesus answered him, 'Because I said to you, I saw you under the fig tree, do you believe? You shall see greater things than these.' And he said to him, 'Truly, truly, I say to you, you will see heaven opened, and the angels of God ascending and descending upon the Son of man' " (Jn. 1:47-51).

It was the custom of pious Jews to pray and meditate under a fig tree, and there Jesus had seen Nathanael before he came into His presence:

"This would indicate that images of people

and things are projected into the imaging chamber of the mind and that by giving them attention one can understand their relation to outer things. Mind readers, clairvoyants, and dreamers have developed this capacity in varying degree. Consciousness is what is concerned with soul unfoldment both primarily, and secondarily and all the way! Forms are always manifestations of ideas. Whoever understands this can interpret the symbols shown him in dreams and visions, but lack of understanding of this law makes one psychic without discernment.

"With this spiritual faculty it is possible for man to penetrate into the 'fourth dimension' or what is usually called the 'kingdom of the heavens' and to discern the trend of the spiritual forces. The angels of God are spiritual forces active in the Sons of God, the spiritually quickened.

"The open and receptive and believing mind can see the things that take place in the Christ Mind, thus transcending the capacity of the unilluminated natural man" (MJ 22-23).

Thus, five of the men who were eventually to become Jesus' apostles—Andrew, John, Peter, Philip, and Nathanael—became acquainted with Him and believed in Him at this time. Apparently, they did not leave their occupations and follow Him, as there is a record of Jesus' calling them later. However, they accompanied Him to Cana of Galilee where all attended a wedding feast. It was at this feast that Jesus performed His first miracle, the changing of water into wine.

A wedding was an event of great importance in Oriental countries and was lavishly celebrated. In wealthy families the festivities often lasted as long as seven days, and even among the poorer classes, one or two days were set aside for celebration. During this particular feast the wine supply was exhausted. As profuse hospitality was a point of honor among the Jews, this was a very embarrassing situation, almost a disgrace. Mary, the mother of Jesus, was among the guests, and she called her son's attention to the deficiency, saying, " 'They have no wine.' And Jesus said to her, 'O woman, what have you to do with me? My hour has not yet come' " (Jn. 2:3-4).

Jesus' seeming rebuke to His mother was not a show of disrespect, as "woman" was a common form of address in those days. His refusal means that when one is functioning in spiritual consciousness, as Jesus was, he is not moved to action until he is directed by the indwelling Christ.

There is a divine fulfillment for every need, but
Spirit cannot be coerced. "My hour has not yet
come," Jesus said, implying that He was not
prompted to act even though He recognized the
lack. Mary willingly acquiesced by saying to the
servants, "Do whatever he tells you" (Jn. 2:5),
and Jesus, who was freed from any interference
from the outer, took command of the situation:

"Now six stone jars were standing there, for
the Jewish rites of purification, each holding
twenty or thirty gallons. Jesus said to them, 'Fill
the jars with water.' And they filled them up to
the brim. He said to them, 'Now draw some out,
and take it to the steward of the feast.' So they
took it. When the steward of the feast tasted the
water now become wine, and did not know
where it came from (though the servants who
had drawn the water knew), the steward of the
feast called the bridegroom and said to him,
'Every man serves the good wine first; and when
men have drunk freely, then the poor wine; but
you have kept the good wine until now' " (Jn.
2:6-10).

A marriage is symbolic of the union of the
consciousness with the indwelling Christ. Before

such a union can take place, the negative state of mind (water) must be transmuted into positive spiritual life (wine).

"The water pots filled to the brim with water by the servants represent the extent to which nature is prepared to fulfill the transformation from negative life to spiritual life through the power of the word of the Master, Jesus" (MJ 25).

The miracle of changing the negative elements in consciousness into spiritual forces is performed in us when, by prayer, we unify our minds with Christ. Then He is in control, and our un-regenerate thoughts and feelings are raised to spiritual heights. Thus, the holy marriage of the soul with Christ is consummated in harmony and joy. As a result, our outer needs are always filled in time to meet the demands (the water was made wine at the right moment). Also, the blessing that comes from Christ is superior to that which the mortal can produce (the ruler of the feast declared the new wine to be the best offered the guests), and it is abundant (more than enough was supplied).

CHAPTER IV

Early Judean Ministry
(First Year)

The time was drawing near for the celebration of the Passover, and Jesus returned to Jerusalem. As He entered the Temple on the first day of the feast, a scene of great confusion met His eyes. The spacious outer court, called the Court of the Gentiles, was the only place in the Temple precincts where Gentile converts were permitted to worship. In this court were stalls where oxen, sheep, and doves were sold for sacrifice. In addition, there were tables where money changers were plying their trade, exchanging foreign coins for Jewish money, as the latter alone was acceptable for the annual Temple tax. As the bargaining for animals and arguments over values went on, loud voices rang out, and the atmosphere that prevailed was certainly not one of reverence.

It is probable that Jesus had witnessed this scene on many occasions and had objected inwardly, but this time the incongruity of it prompted Him to take action.

"And making a whip of cords, he drove them

all, with the sheep and oxen, out of the temple; and he poured out the coins of the money-changers and overturned their tables. And he told those who sold the pigeons, 'Take these things away; you shall not make my Father's house a house of trade' '' (Jn. 2:15-16).

The Temple represents the body, the house of Spirit. The body should be maintained as a fit place of worship, and its sanctity should be recognized. Often, however, our mental and emotional states are far from devout, and our bodies become infested with undesirable conditions that are evidence of greedy, material thoughts.

"When we throw the light of Spirit into the subconscious courts of the body temple, we find queer and often startling conditions there. One would hardly expect to see butcher stalls and money-changers in a temple built for the worship of God, yet similar conditions exist in all of us.

"So the body temple must be cleansed; it is the house of God ('for we are a temple of the living God'), and it should be put in order. The first step in this cleansing process is to recognize its need. The next step is the 'scourge of small

cords' (AV): to formulate the word or statement
of denial. When we deny in general terms we
cleanse the consciousness, but secret sins may yet
lurk in the inner parts. The words that most easily reach these hidden errors are not great ones,
such as 'I am one with Almightiness; my environment is God' but small, definite statements
that cut like whipcords into the sensuous, fleshly
mentality'' (MJ 28-29).

Those in charge of the Temple were incensed
at what they considered Jesus' temerity in cleansing the court, and asked Him by what right He
did this thing. His reply probably seemed rather
irrelevant to them, for He said, ''Destroy this
temple, and in three days I will raise it up'' (Jn.
2:19). Because forty-six years had been required
to build the Temple, Jesus' answer, then, was
difficult for the Temple leaders to understand.
''What could he mean?'' they inquired. ''But
he spoke of the temple of his body'' (Jn. 2:21).
This was Jesus' first prediction that His body was
to be resurrected.

''Man's ability to preserve his body from destruction is the proof that he has mastered his
mind. So long as our body shows signs of decay it

is evident that we have not cast out of the inner realms the 'thought butchers' that for a sacrifice kill doves, sheep, oxen, and goats. The allusion here is to the destructive thoughts lying deep in the consciousness at the very issue of life'' (MJ 32).

The three days that Jesus specified symbolize man's threefold nature—spirit, soul, and body. When one functions in spiritual consciousness, he has control over soul and body, and knows that the body can be resurrected ("in three days I will raise it up").

During His stay in Jerusalem, Jesus wrought miracles, and "many believed in his name" (Jn. 2:23).

The Pharisees were the largest and most influential of the Jewish sects, and their ideal was to live in full accord with the will of God as it is revealed in both the written and the oral law. (The written law was the Mosaic law contained in the Old Testament; the oral law consisted of a great many explanations and interpretations of the written law that had been made by famous scribes and rabbis.)

Characteristic of the Pharisees was their religious zeal. Insisting on a strict observance of all

ceremonial requirements, they were considered
very pious by the masses of the people and
exerted much influence over them. The great
fault of the Pharisees lay in the fact that they
placed so much stress on the outer forms of worship that they lost sight of the inner spirit of it.
By the beginning of the Christian era the Pharisees had, as a class, become narrow, dogmatic,
self-righteous, and conceited. Charles Fillmore
states:

"In individual consciousness Pharisees represent thoughts that arise out of the subconsciousness, binding man to external forms of religion
without giving him understanding of their real
meaning" (MD 521).

"It is the Pharisee in us that causes us to love
the forms and ceremonies of religion. It is the
Pharisee in us that refuses to go deep into the
consciousness and cleanse the inner man. It is the
Pharisee in us that is ambitious for temporal
honors and loves to be saluted with high-sound-
ing titles. It is the pharisaical thought that exalts
and sustains personality.

"We can overcome the Pharisee in ourselves
by receiving continuously new inspiration from

the original fount of being within us, and by
refusing to be bound by old, effete, religious
thoughts'' (MD 522).

During His stay in Jerusalem, Jesus was visited
by Nicodemus, a leading Pharisee, and ''a ruler
of the Jews'' (Jn. 3:1). This last phrase indicates
that Nicodemus was a member of the Jewish supreme court, called the Sanhedrin (see Chap.
X). Nicodemus came to see Jesus ''by night,''
indicating that he wished his visit to be in secret.
Spiritually, the night visit signifies that Nicodemus had intellectual but not spiritual understanding. Yet, in Nicodemus there was a perception of higher things than he had heretofore
known, and he proved his willingness to learn by
seeking out Jesus. Even though we may have
been reared with dogmatic concepts of religion,
spiritual light will be shown us if we seek for it.

Revealing his instinctive regard for Jesus,
Nicodemus addressed Him as Rabbi, and said,
''We know that you are a teacher come from
God; for no one can do these signs that you do,
unless God is with him'' (Jn. 3:2). Before he had
a chance to say more, Jesus answered the question that was in His visitor's mind:

" 'Truly, truly, I say to you, unless one is born anew, he cannot see the kingdom of God.' Nicodemus said to him, 'How can a man be born when he is old?' . . . Jesus answered, 'Truly, truly, I say to you, unless one is born of water and the Spirit, he cannot enter the kingdom of God. That which is born of the flesh is flesh, and that which is born of the Spirit is spirit. Do not marvel that I said to you, "You must be born anew." The wind blows where it wills, and you hear the sound of it, but you do not know whence it comes or whither it goes; so it is with every one who is born of the Spirit' " (Jn. 3:3-8).

Our innate desire is to progress spiritually; we want to "see the kingdom of God." But this is not possible until we are "born anew." We are born of the flesh, that is, we are living in a world where the sense or mortal consciousness governs, and in the main, our desires and interests have to do with the satisfaction of the sense nature or with the seemingly required routines of life. When we wish to be born of Spirit, we must be willing and eager to come into a higher state of consciousness. Jesus defined the new birth as being "born of water and the Spirit." Water cleanses and purifies. Water baptism signifies repentance or a turning from the sense nature, a denial of destructive thoughts and emotions.

"To be 'born of the Spirit' is to come into the consciousness of divine law and to lift the whole man into a new life of harmony and order by affirmative prayer" (MD 482-83).

Spirit is not a force that we have anything to do with in the sense of creating it. Like the wind, it "blows where it wills," and we are aware of it. He that is born of Spirit does not fully comprehend how the change came about or when but he knows full well that he is a different person.

"The new birth is simply the realization by man of his spiritual identity, with the fullness of power and glory that follows" (MJ 37-38).

Nicodemus did not understand this and asked, "How can these things be?" Before answering, Jesus asked Nicodemus how it was that he, being a teacher of Israel, could be ignorant of spiritual things. But we know that many people who make a study of religious teachings are unaware of the action of Spirit. Continuing His teaching, Jesus said, "No one has ascended into heaven but he who descended from heaven, the Son of man" (Jn. 3:13).

"There is but one real man, the ideal or spiritual man that God created. Jesus was explaining to Nicodemus the evolution of this spiritual man from his ideal to his manifest state. Man is fundamentally spiritual and so remains throughout his various manifestations. He comes out of heaven, manifests himself as a personality in the earth, and returns to heaven. . . . Faith in Spirit and the ultimate dominance of the good in man will finally restore him to the heaven from which he descended" (MJ 37).

It is our privilege and responsibility to evolve from mortal to spiritual consciousness. "And as Moses lifted up the serpent in the wilderness, so must the Son of man be lifted up, that whoever believes in him may have eternal life" (Jn. 3:14-15). We are given the power to do this by our Creator: "For God so loved the world that he gave his only Son, that whosoever believes in him should not perish but have eternal life" (Jn. 3:16).

The "only Son" is the Christ within all of us,

the spirit of God that is the very core of our being. God is love, and He gave of Himself to His offspring. We should acknowledge our divine heritage as well as believe in the divinity of Jesus. "This belief must then lead us to a desire and an effort to attain our inheritance, because then we know that there is no other thing in the universe worth striving for" (MJ 38).

Jesus explained that He, as God's Son, came into the world to save people, not to judge them, and:

"He who believes in him is not condemned; he who does not believe is condemned already, because he has not believed in the name of the only Son of God" (Jn. 3:18).

Salvation from sin, sickness, and sorrow begins when we have faith in Jesus as the Way-Shower and Savior. Through the application of His teachings, we are saved from the dire effects of transgression. Jesus showed us the way of righteousness. Righteousness actually means the right or correct use of universal Principle. When we do not follow Him, we make the mistakes that belong to the human level of living and are "judged already"; we pay the penalty for deviating from the law of God, which rules supreme in the universe.

"And this is the judgment, that the light has come into the world, and men loved darkness rather than light, because their deeds were evil. For every one who does evil hates the light, and does not come to the light, lest his deeds should be exposed. But he who does what is true comes to the light, that it may be clearly seen that his deeds have been wrought in God" (Jn. 3:19-21).

Before a spiritual awakening we dwell in the ignorance of darkness of mortal concepts. As a result, our works are evil, and we "hate" the light. We begin to develop spiritually when we come "to the light." The way of righteousness is perceived, and we endeavor to follow it. We think differently; we act more worthily, and our works bear evidence that they "have been wrought in God."

For a time Jesus remained in Judea preaching near the place where John the Baptist was conducting his ministry. After John was imprisoned by Herod Antipas, Jesus returned to Galilee. To make the trip He had to go through Samaria, a section of Palestine lying between Judea and

Galilee.

The Judean Jews would have no dealings with the Samaritans, for they considered them of lower quality racially and religiously. The city of Samaria, from which the province took its name, was the capital of the old kingdom of Israel that had been conquered by Sargon II of Assyria in 722 B.C. Sargon deported thousands of the Hebrew inhabitants and imported various foreign tribes. During the passage of years the Hebrews who had been left in Israel intermarried with the foreigners, thus producing a mixed race. The religion of the Samaritans was similar to that of the Jews, for they accepted the Mosaic law and claimed Abraham as their ancestor. However, the Samaritans rejected the great Hebrew prophets and, both in ideals and practices, were deemed inferior to the pure-blooded Jews. A Judean Jew felt himself vastly superior to a Samaritan and would not pass through the latter's territory if he could avoid it. Not so with Jesus. He felt that all people had equal standing in God's sight.

Samaria represents a mixed consciousness, partly worldly and partly religious, that results in a confused state of mind. Each of us in developing spiritually has to "pass through Samaria"

(Jn. 4:4). And we may do so by allowing the Christ to instruct us.

When Jesus reached the Samaritan village of Sychar, He sat down beside a well to rest while His companions entered the village to buy food. A woman came to the well to draw water, and Jesus asked her to give Him a drink. It was not customary for a Jew to ask anything of a Samaritan, and the woman's surprise must have been apparent. Jesus said:

" 'If you knew the gift of God, and who it is that is saying to you, "Give me a drink," you would have asked him and he would have given you living water.' The woman said to him, 'Sir, you have nothing to draw with, and the well is deep; where do you get that living water? Are you greater than our father Jacob, who gave us the well, and drank from it himself, and his sons, and his cattle?' Jesus said to her, 'Every one who drinks of this water will thirst again, but whoever drinks of the water that I shall give him will never thirst; the water that I shall give him will become in him a spring of water welling up to eternal life' " (Jn. 4:10-14).

The Samaritan woman represents the soul that

has not yet been spiritually quickened:

"But the soul must have Truth, and Christ recognizes the soul as worthy; hence this wonderful lesson of John 4:9-26 given to one auditor. The soul draws its life from both the earthly side of existence (Jacob's well) and the spiritual (the Jew), but is destined to draw from a higher fount, omnipotent Spirit. Jesus asked the woman for a drink, which indicates the universality of the spiritual life, present in the Samaritan woman as well as in Jesus.

" 'The gift of God' to man is eternal life. The soul informed of this truth asks the Father for the manifestation of this life, and there gushes forth a never-failing stream. But where sense consciousness is dominant the soul is slow to see the realities of ideas, thoughts, and words; the sight is fixed on material ways and means: 'Thou hast nothing to draw with . . . whence then hast thou that living water?' This is a fair setting forth of the status of the questioning ones of this day who ask the explanation of spiritual things on a material basis" (MJ 47-48).

In spite of the woman's doubt, Jesus offered to give her "living water" (spiritual inspiration) that would be an eternal blessing. The woman then said, "Sir, give me this water, that I may not thirst, nor come here to draw" (Jn. 4:15). Everyone longs for satisfaction but does not know how to attain it. Jesus called the woman's attention to the fact that He knew she was leading an immoral life and that this would deter her spiritual progress. She showed that she was willing to learn a higher way when she asked a question concerning worship:

" 'Our fathers worshiped on this mountain; and you say that in Jerusalem is the place where men ought to worship.' Jesus said to her, 'Woman, believe me, the hour is coming when neither on this mountain nor in Jerusalem will you worship the Father. You worship what you do not know; we worship what we know, for salvation is from the Jews. But the hour is coming, and now is, when the true worshipers will worship the Father in spirit and truth, for such the Father seeks to worship him. God is Spirit, and those who worship him must worship in spirit and truth' " (Jn. 4:20-24).

Before we are attuned to Spirit we consider places and things as paramount, even in worshiping God. The Samaritan woman could not understand why the Jews believed that Jerusalem was the only proper place to worship. Spiritually interpreted, the Jews represent a higher concept of God; hence, Jesus' words, "Salvation is from the Jews." Yet the time comes when we need a more spiritual understanding of God and how to worship Him:

"To worship God truly we must know where He is and how to approach Him. If, as many teach, God lives in heaven, and heaven is located somewhere in the skies, we have a consciousness of separation from Him, and our approach to Him is uncertain.

"But when we know the truth about God, that He is an omnipresent Spirit manifesting Himself to our mind when we think of Him as one with us in Spirit and responding to our every thought, then we know Him as He is" (MJ 46).

The woman avowed that she believed in the coming of the Messiah who will show us all things, and Jesus replied, "I who speak to you am he" (Jn. 4:26). This was His first revelation to anyone of His true identity.

When Jesus' companions returned from the

village they were astonished to find Him speaking to a woman, and especially a Samaritan. True, she had not understood the spiritual import of His words; nevertheless, she was impressed by them and particularly impressed by His knowledge of her personal life. She hastened to the village and reported her unusual experience. "Can this be the Christ?" (Jn. 4:29), she queried. Many of the villagers then started out to find Jesus.

In the meantime, Jesus' companions urged Him to eat the food they had brought:

"But he said to them, 'I have food to eat of which you do not know. . . . My food is to do the will of him who sent me, and to accomplish his work. Do you not say, "There are yet four months, then comes the harvest"? I tell you, lift up your eyes, and see how the fields are already white for harvest. He who reaps receives wages, and gathers fruit for eternal life, so that sower and reaper may rejoice together. For here the saying holds true, "One sows and another reaps." I sent you to reap that for which you did not labor; others have labored, and you have entered into their labor' " (Jn. 4:32-38).

Spiritual man (Jesus) draws on the substance of divine ideas that nourish and sustain the consciousness. Jesus' ideal and mission was to do the Father's will, and in speaking God's word to the woman of Samaria, He was fulfilling His mission. Hence, He felt a sense of satisfaction and completeness. Man lives not by bread alone, but "by every word that proceeds from the mouth of God" (Mt. 4:4). The divine word is revealed to us when we love God and share His freeing Truth with others. Those who are still expressing in human consciousness (Jesus' companions) are not aware of this inner nourishment. They think that we are dependent on the outer (planting and harvesting) for food. To one of higher vision, the fields are "already white for harvest," meaning that the pure substance of Spirit, which is the source of both inner and outer sustenance, is now at hand and can be appropriated by all. The one who knows God and does His will "reaps" and gathers fruit "for eternal life"; that is, feels the quickening of Spirit and experiences the joy of expressing divine attributes. Jesus had made this spiritual attainment ("one sows"), and He was willing to share His understanding with His companions ("another reaps"), so that both He and they might "rejoice together."

Jesus was ever ready to give the Truth to all alike, be they publicans or sinners, Jews or Samaritans, proving that salvation is for anyone who will accept Christ and have faith in the spiritual kingdom. As Jesus finished speaking, the people of Samaria approached and "asked him to stay with them; and he stayed there two days. And many more believed because of his word" (Jn. 4:40-41).

CHAPTER V

Great Galilean Ministry

(Second Year)

Galilee, the little country made famous through Jesus of Nazareth, consists for the most part of an elevated plateau, dropping on the east to the lovely harp-shaped Sea of Galilee (also called Gennesaret and Chinnereth but now known as the Lake of Tiberias). The Jordan River flows into the Sea of Galilee from the north and from it toward the Dead Sea in Judea. In Jesus' time Galilee was a fertile land yielding abundant crops. The sea teemed with fish, and many Galileans were fishermen. Large towns and villages dotted the province, the three chief cities being Capernaum, Bethsaida, and Chorazin. The main highways from Egypt to Syria and from Phoenicia to Persia passed through Galilee, making it a center of traffic.

It was in this setting that Jesus began the second year of His ministry, sometimes referred to as the Galilean ministry, and also as the Year of Popularity. His activity was now incessant, His service was largely to the multitudes, and before the year ended Jesus' fame was ringing throughout the length and breadth of Palestine. When Jesus arrived in His home territory, "the Galileans welcomed him, having seen all that he had done in Jerusalem at the feast" (Jn. 4:45).

Jesus went first to Cana, where He had previously performed the miracle of turning the water to wine at a wedding party. It was here that a nobleman besought Jesus to heal his son who was at the point of death. The nobleman felt that there was an immediate need of action and that it would be necessary for Jesus to accompany him to his son's bedside. But Jesus, well aware that God's power is omnipresent, told the nobleman, "Go; your son will live" (Jn. 4:50). Apparently the nobleman was impressed, for he hastened home, where he was met by servants bearing the glad news that his son had been healed, and at the very hour when Jesus had spoken the word. It is easy to imagine the nobleman's joy when he heard the good news, and from that time on, he and his household believed in the teachings of Jesus.

In the incident of the nobleman's son we have the first detailed account of an individual healing that Jesus performed. Besides a number of statements to the effect that He healed many people, evidently in groups where He was teaching, more than twenty instances of individual healing are given in The Gospels. In most instances Jesus was in the presence of the sufferer, but there are several accounts of healings that were accomplished from a distance, such as the one related above.

The secret of spiritual healing is the recognition and acknowledgment of wholeness in the person who is expressing a physical limitation, and much effective healing is being done today through earnest prayer. It is not necessary for the sick person to be in the presence of the one or ones who are praying.

In the majority of the individual accounts of healings, Jesus merely spoke the word such as, "Be clean" (Mt. 8:3). In several instances, however, He performed an act, as when He "made clay of the spittle," anointed the eyes of the man born blind, and told him to wash in the pool of Siloam (Jn. 9:1-7). Jesus' course in doing something for the afflicted person, and telling him to do something for himself, seems to have been for the purpose of strengthening the man's faith. It is occasionally effective in our healing work today to combine prayer and action. Healing can only result when faith enters in, but often the act tends to increase faith.

Among Jesus' healings there is at least one where a partial healing preceded a complete cure (Mk. 8:22-25). In this case, Jesus put His hands on the eyes of the blind man, and the man reported that he saw men "like trees, walking." Jesus again placed His hands on the man's eyes, and his sight was wholly restored. This should encourage us. Often our own healings and those for whom we pray are gradual, but they can be instantaneous, as they generally were when Jesus spoke the word of wholeness. In the event our faith is not sufficient to accept a complete restoration immediately, we should understand that an improvement in the condition is evidence of the activity of Spirit. Our part is to continue to pray until the full healing is accomplished. Charles Fillmore says:

"Ability to pick up the life current and through it perpetually to vitalize the body is based on the right relation of ideas, thoughts, and words. These mental impulses start currents of energy that form and also stimulate molecules and cells already formed, producing life, strength, and animation where inertia and impotence was the dominant appearance. This was and is the healing method of Jesus" (JC 5).

The healings that Jesus performed, covering as they did every sort of physical and mental deficiency, are considered miracles. To them should be added the three occasions on which He raised people from the dead: the son of the widow of Nain (Lk. 7:11-17), the daughter of Jairus (Mt. 9:18-26), and Lazarus (Jn. 11:1-46). In addition, He performed other miracles of a general nature, such as healing the epileptic child (Mt. 17:14), multiplying the loaves and fishes to feed five thousand (Mt. 14:13-23), and walking on the water (Mt. 14:24-36).

What is a miracle? One dictionary defines a miracle as "an event or effect in the physical world deviating from the known laws of nature, or transcending our knowledge of these laws." According to this definition, Jesus did perform miracles. Many Christians contend that miraculous power was given only to Jesus and His immediate followers. Metaphysically, a miracle is explained as being the outcome of man's obedience to divine law. Jesus gave His whole attention to God and thus established a union with the creative life within Him. Being master of Himself, He had dominion over all conditions and asserted the authority that was given to man in the beginning. He said, however, "He who

believes in me," that is, believes in the reality of
spiritual man, "Truly, truly, I say to you, he who
believes in me will also do the works that I do;
and greater works than these will he do" (Jn.
14:12). Jesus' real mission was to teach us to follow Him by lifting our consciousness from the
sense level to a spiritual level. Every person is
made in the image and likeness of God. When
we realize this, and live in harmony with the indwelling Christ, we are able to use our power to
bring about conditions that may seem miraculous to one who is functioning in human consciousness.

Jesus did not perform His great works (miracles) in an effort to draw attention to Himself
and thus gain a following; neither were they
done to satisfy the curiosity of the people. They
were done to glorify God and to bring about
wholeness. The Pharisees frequently demanded a
sign that He (Jesus) was sent of God, and Jesus
consistently refused, saying, "An evil and
adulterous generation seeks for a sign, but no
sign shall be given to it except the sign of Jonah"
(Mt. 16:4). He demanded faith from people
whom He healed, and His works were done to
help humankind. He often "charged them to
tell no one" (Mk. 7:36). Such deeds were impos-

sible to hide even in individual cases. Many of the miracles were performed in the presence of groups. Therefore, with each deed of mercy His fame increased.

From Cana, where He had healed the nobleman's son, Jesus went to His hometown of Nazareth. On the Sabbath He attended the local synagogue. Every city or town of any size had one or more synagogues where services were held regularly. The services were under the jurisdiction of elders, and the chief officer was known as the Ruler of the Synagogue. In contrast to the elaborate ceremonies in the Temple at Jerusalem, which only priests could conduct, the service in a synagogue was simple, and frequently a layman was invited to participate. On this occasion Jesus was asked to take part, and He was handed the book of the prophet Isaiah from which to read. He selected these significant verses:

"The Spirit of the Lord is upon me,
 because he has anointed me to preach good
  news to the poor.
 He has sent me to proclaim release to the
  captives
 and recovering of sight to the blind,
 to set at liberty those who are oppressed,

to proclaim the acceptable year of the Lord.''
—Luke 4:18-19

Handing the book back to the clerk, Jesus sat
down to deliver His sermon, a customary practice
among the Jews. ''And he began to say to them,
'Today this scripture has been fulfilled in your
hearing' '' (Lk. 4:21). This was equivalent to
saying that He was the Messiah prophesied by
Isaiah and that He was to fulfill the works of the
anointed of God. This announcement so amazed
His hearers that they began to murmur, ''Is not
this Joseph's son?'' (Lk. 4:22) They could not
conceive of one of their own neighbors as being
the promised Messiah. Jesus' defense of His position filled them with wrath. They took hold of
Him and led Him to the brow of a hill from
which they intended to cast Him down. ''But
passing through the midst of them he went
away'' (Lk. 4:30). This eluding of the angry
crowd was a most unusual occurrence and is
thought-provoking. Jesus did not have to fight
His way out of this difficult situation. Apparently, it was handled calmly and easily. He trusted
His Father to care for Him in His time of need.
We can do likewise and we do not have to know
just how we shall be protected.

Perhaps it was this rejection at Nazareth that led Jesus to select Capernaum as the headquarters for His Galilean ministry. As He was walking by the Sea of Galilee, He called four men to be His apostles—Peter, Andrew, James, and John, the last two being the sons of Zebedee. Jesus' invitation was, "Follow me, and I will make you fishers of men" (Mt. 4:19). Three of these men, Andrew, Peter, and John, were with Jesus at least part of the time in His early Judean ministry; yet it was at the time of this calling that they left their homes and occupations and "followed him." The Gospels give an account of Jesus' calling only one other apostle. This was Matthew, a publican and a Jew, who collected taxes for the Roman government. Those who served in the capacity of publican were despised by the Jews, for the position lent itself to corruption, oppression, and abuse. But Matthew, at the call of Jesus, "left everything, and rose and followed him" (Lk. 5:28).

Jesus performed many healings in Capernaum and the surrounding territory, and these, together with His teachings, attracted the attention of the scribes and Pharisees. The scribes, most of whom were Pharisees, were Jewish scholars and professional interpreters of the law, sometimes referred to as lawyers or doctors of the law. The scribes copied the Hebrew Scriptures into Aramaic, the language generally spoken in Palestine. In addition, they made new regulations, called in The Gospels "the tradition of the elders" (Mt. 15:2).

At the start of Jesus' ministry in Galilee, the scribes and Pharisees seemed to be genuinely interested in what He said and did. "And they were astonished at his teaching, for he taught them as one who had authority, and not as the scribes" (Mk. 1:22). It was the custom of the scribes to read the law and to quote profusely from the writings of learned rabbis. Here was a man speaking on His own authority. They listened and marveled when He healed a demoniac (Mk. 1:21-28) and a leper (Mk.1:40-45). But Jesus soon antagonized them by healing on the Sabbath. To them this constituted a violation of their law, for a rigid observance of Sabbath rules and regulations was sacred to them. Jesus maintained, "It is lawful to do good on the sabbath" (Mt. 12:12). When the Pharisees objected to Jesus' disciples plucking corn as they went through the grainfields on the Sabbath, He declared, "The sabbath was made for man, not man for the sabbath" (Mk. 2:27). They considered it sacrilegious when He said to a paralytic whom He healed, "Your sins are forgiven" (Mt. 9:2). They believed that only God can forgive sins. Jesus' reply was, "The Son of man has authority on earth to forgive sins" (Mt. 9:6).

"Forgiveness really means the giving up of something. When you forgive yourself, you cease doing the thing that you ought not to do. Jesus was correct in assuming that man has power to forgive sin. Sin is a falling short of the divine law, and repentance and forgiveness are the only means that man has of getting out of sin and its effect and coming into harmony with the law. . . . Some mental attitude, some train of mental energy, must be transformed. We forgive sin in ourselves every time we resolve to think and act according to the divine law" (JC 58-59).

In still other ways, Jesus' actions antagonized the Jewish leaders. To them it was inconceivable that a religious teacher would associate with publicans and sinners. Yet Jesus had feasted with them at a dinner given in His honor by Matthew, the publican, and had defended His position by saying, "Those who are well have no need of a physician, but those who are sick. . . . I came

not to call the righteous, but sinners'' (Mt.
9:12-13). He well knew that His mission was to
the outcasts as well as other needy people.

The Pharisees were also displeased that neither
Jesus nor His disciples fulfilled the requirements
of the oral law as it applied to fasting. Even the
disciples of John the Baptist, who was himself
somewhat revolutionary in his preaching, complied with this provision. Jesus reminded those
who asked for an explanation that it was not wise
to sew a new piece of cloth on an old garment
nor put new wine into old wineskins. This implied that the new teachings that He was giving
could not fit into the patterns of old beliefs to
which the Pharisees had become bound (Mt.
9:16-17). Metaphysically, the Pharisees represent
a phase of consciousness that adheres to the outer
observance of religion, and Jesus represents the
higher consciousness that knows itself to be one
with Spirit.

During the second year of His ministry Jesus
went to Jerusalem to attend a feast, possibly the
Passover. At the pool of Bethesda Jesus healed a
man who had been lame for thirty-eight years
(Jn. 5:1-47). On this occasion the Pharisees were
doubly offended, for Jesus not only healed on
the Sabbath but He called God His Father. To

them, such action was blasphemy. To this charge Jesus replied, "Truly, truly, I say to you, the Son can do nothing of his own accord, but only what he sees the Father doing . . . . For the Father loves the Son, and shows him all that he himself is doing . . . . For as the Father raises the dead and gives them life, so also the Son gives life to whom he will" (Jn. 5:19-21). Jesus understood that the Son (conscious self) can do nothing unless unified with the Father (super-consciousness or Christ self). However, when this union has been made, one is aware of the power of the indwelling Christ and can speak the healing word.

The Pharisees, symbolizing the attitude of mind that loves the outer observance of religion, could not heal. They did not understand that they, too, had access to the Spirit of truth within them and that they could and should claim oneness with it. Jesus knew He was one with the Father, and He spoke in that consciousness. To those who were still on a lower level of thought, such a realization as Jesus had was a mystery of which they were skeptical, critical, and antagonistic. In His contests with the Pharisees, Jesus was always able to silence them temporarily with His logical replies, but a smoldering anger and resentment stirred within them which was to burst into violent hostility later on.

After Jesus returned to Galilee He was followed by great crowds that pressed around Him. Word of His marvelous healings had traveled like wildfire through Palestine and even to Phoenicia. Many who were ill came to Him, along with the throngs that were attracted by His teaching. "And he told his disciples to have a boat ready for him because of the crowd, lest they should crush him" (Mk. 3:9). The little boat was to become His favorite pulpit, and from it He taught and healed the multitude that gathered on the shore of the sea.

Finally, from the many who followed Him, Jesus selected twelve men to be His apostles. He had previously accepted seven of them (Andrew, Peter, James and John [sons of Zebedee], Philip, Bartholomew, and Matthew). Judas Iscariot was the only apostle who was a Judean; all the others were Galileans. Jesus had prayed all night before making this important decision. Luke tells us:

"And when it was day, he called his disciples, and chose from them twelve, whom he named apostles; Simon, whom he named Peter, and Andrew his brother, and James and John, and Philip, and Bartholomew, and Matthew, and

Thomas, and James the son of Alphaeus, and Simon who was called the Zealot, and Judas the son of James, and Judas Iscariot, who became a traitor'' (Lk. 6:13-16).

Metaphysically, the Apostles represent the twelve spiritual qualities or powers within man. These powers have their origin in the super-conscious or spiritual phase of mind, but they function through the subconscious mind. Charles Fillmore states:

"When Jesus had attained a certain soul development, He called His twelve apostles to Him. This means that when man is developing out of mere personal consciousness into spiritual consciousness, he begins to train deeper and larger powers . . . . Where before his powers have worked in the personal, now they begin to expand and work in the universal" (TM 15).

It is our privilege to call these great faculties (Apostles) from the mortal, where they have been expressing, to the spiritual where their work becomes much more effectual, and each is of vital importance and necessary to the unfoldment of the Christ self. Jesus chose the Twelve just before He gave the Sermon on the Mount. Before we can fully comprehend the vital and lofty meaning of the Sermon, these twelve spiritual powers within us must be quickened.

The apostle Peter represents faith. "We begin our religious experience, our unity with Divine Mind, by having faith in that mind as omnipresent, all-wise, all-loving, all-powerful Spirit" (TM 17). Faith is thus the essential foundation for the building of a spiritual consciousness. At first faith is wavering and changeable, as was Peter when he became frightened while walking on the water, and when, in fear, he denied knowing Jesus.

"You must teach Peter to concentrate. Teach him to center on true words. It is through him that you feed your sheep, your other faculties. Keep him right at his task. He is inquisitive, impulsive, and dictatorial, when not firmly directed. When he questions your dominion and tries to dictate the movements of your other powers, put him in line with, 'What is that to thee? follow thou me' " (MD 518).

If we continue to affirm our faith in God, a steadfast faith becomes established in us and is the rock upon which our church (spiritual consciousness) is built.

The apostle Andrew represents strength. In people strength is thought of primarily as physical stamina, to which we add strength of purpose and moral character as we develop. When it is raised to a spiritual level strength enables a person to overcome human might. David was able to slay Goliath because he had the strength of Spirit.

"Be steadfast, strong, and steady in thought, and you will establish strength in mind and in body. Never let the thought of weakness enter your consciousness, but always ignore the suggestion and affirm yourself to be a tower of strength, within and without" (TM 38).

The apostle James, the son of Zebedee, represents wisdom and judgment. James is the faculty in us by which we weigh a matter and come to a conclusion. When judgment is divorced from wisdom its conclusions are faulty and lead to condemnation and criticism. Through the faithful affirmation of wisdom and good judgment, the spiritual aspect of this power comes into activity.

"When we awaken to the reality of our being, the light begins to break upon us from within and we know the truth; this is the quickening of our James or judgment faculty. When this quickening occurs, we find ourselves discriminating between the good and the evil. We no longer accept the race standards or the teachings of the worldly wise, but we 'judge righteous judgment'; we know with an inner intuition, and we judge men and events from a new viewpoint" (TM 44).

The apostle John represents love. John is also the son of Zebedee and, therefore, the brother of James. Wisdom and love are closely related and should function in unison. Wisdom may be harsh without love, and love may be foolish without wisdom. When spiritual love is quickened it becomes a healing, harmonizing force in the life of an individual. Jesus summed up the Ten Commandments in two great ones that are based on love: " 'And you shall love the Lord your God with all your heart, and with all your soul, and with all your mind, and with all your strength.' The second is this, 'You shall love your neighbor as yourself' " (Mk. 12:30-31). We recognize God as law through the wisdom or judgment faculty, James; we fulfill the law through the love faculty, John.

Philip represents power. Power is the ability to do, to perform, and to accomplish. In unredeemed man, power is expressed in selfish ways to gain what man wishes to have in the material world. The power God has given us is the dominion and mastery over ourselves. "He who rules his spirit [is more powerful] than he who takes a city" (Prov. 16:32).

"In the process of regeneration the consciousness of power ebbs and flows, because the old and the new tides of thought act and react in the conscious and subconscious realms of mind. However, when a disciple realizes his unity with Omnipotence he is but little disturbed by the changes that go on in his mind and his body. He knows that his spiritual dominion is established, and this firm conviction expresses itself in firm words. . . . Jesus said, 'Heaven and earth shall pass away, but my words shall not pass away.' Here is evidence of spiritual power united with the idea of eternity" (MD 525).

The risen Jesus said to His Apostles, "You shall receive power when the Holy Spirit has come upon you'' (Acts 1:8). When the spiritual consciousness is quickened, there is an inflow of power from on high (the Christ center of our being).

Bartholomew, called Nathanael in the Gospel of John, represents imagination. All visible forms have their origin in the imagination, and it is through the activity of this faculty that the formless takes form, thus molding our bodies and the conditions of our lives. The Lord instructed Moses to make all things ''after the pattern for them, which is being shown you on the mountain'' (Ex. 25:40). The mountain represents the spiritual consciousness; therefore, we are to make (image) in accord with our highest realizations. It is our right to call on Bartholomew when things look dark, and through the faculty of the spiritual imagination we see the silver lining of the cloud—health instead of sickness, opulence instead of lack, peace instead of inharmony.

Thomas represents understanding. In the human consciousness understanding is related to intellect but it is attuned to wisdom in spiritual consciousness. We should have an intuitive knowledge that is based on spiritual perception, and not on reason.

"When we discover in ourselves a flow of thought that seems to have been evolved independently of the reasoning process, we are often puzzled about its origin and its safety as a guide. In its beginnings this seemingly strange source of knowledge is often turned aside as a daydream; again it seems a distant voice, an echo of something that we have heard and forgotten. One should give attention to this unusual and usually faint whispering of Spirit in man. It is not of the intellect . . . . It is the development, in man, of a greater capacity to know himself and to understand the purpose of creation. . . . It is accredited [in the Bible] as coming from the heart. The nature of the process is not explained; one who is in the devotional stage of unfoldment need not know all the complex movements of the mind in order to get the message of the Lord. It is enough to know that the understanding is opened in both head and heart when man gives himself wholly to the Lord" (TM 90).

Matthew represents the will. The will is the executive power of the mind and is the focal point around which all our actions center. It is the power to act decisively. Man is a free agent who possesses and uses this faculty.

"The will always enters into man's decision. The will makes the final choice to give up all and follow Jesus. . . . The will has been given over to the thought of accumulation by imposition on external resources (tax gatherer). In the regeneration the will is converted, and is taught by prayer and meditation how to stabilize the universal substance. . . . When the individual will has become a disciple of the Christ, spiritual I AM, the schooling of the man begins" (MD 434).

The highest office of the will is to unify itself with divine will. This is exemplified in Jesus' prayer, "Not my will, but thine, be done" (Lk. 22:42).

James, the son of Alphaeus, represents law and order. Order is termed "heaven's first law," and Paul cautions, "But all things should be done decently and in order" (1 Cor. 14:40).

"Man can never exercise dominion until he knows who and what he is and, knowing, brings forth that knowledge into the external by exercising it in divine order, which is mind, idea, and manifestation" (TM 113).

Jesus outlined the orderly procedure for our

spiritual progress when He said, "First the blade, then the ear, then the full grain in the ear" (Mk. 4:28). The blade represents the period when Truth is being implanted in the mind; the ear signifies the growth and development of spiritual ideas; and the full grain in the ear is the manifestation or bringing forth of these ideas. In our unfoldment we are prone to disregard this orderly sequence and attempt to jump from blade to full grain. This is as impossible as trying to leap from infancy to adulthood. In all ways growth should be orderly if it is to follow the harmonious laws of the universe. As regards both our inner and outer lives we need to understand God's law and cooperate with it in an orderly manner.

Simon the Zealot represents zeal.

"Zeal is the mighty force that incites the winds, the tides, the storms; it urges the planet on its course, and spurs the ant to great exertion. To be without zeal is to be without the zest of living. Zeal and enthusiasm incite to glorious achievement in every aim and ideal that the mind conceives. Zeal is the impulse to go forward, the urge behind all things. Without zeal stagnation, inertia, death would prevail throughout the universe. The man without zeal is like an engine without steam or an electric motor without a current. Energy is zeal in motion, and energy is the forerunner of every effect'' (TM 130).

We should not repress zeal but, on the other hand, care should be taken to keep zeal balanced with wisdom. Paul says, ''They have a zeal for God, but it is not enlightened'' (Rom. 10:2).

''One may even become so zealous for the spread of Truth as to bring on nervous prostration. 'Take time to be holy.' Turn a portion of your zeal to do God's will to the establishing of His kingdom within you. Do not put all your enthusiasm into teaching, preaching, healing, and helping others; help yourself. Many enthusiastic spiritual workers have let their zeal to demonstrate Truth to others rob them of the power to demonstrate Truth for themselves. Do not let your zeal run away with your judgment'' (TM 132-133).

Thaddaeus, the son of James, called Judas in Luke's gospel, represents renunciation. To renounce means to relinquish or eliminate. In the process of spiritual unfoldment we must renounce many false beliefs and destructive emotions.

"It is just as necessary that one should learn to let go of thoughts, conditions, and substances in consciousness, body, and affairs, when they have served their purpose and one no longer needs them, as it is that one should lay hold of new ideas and new substances to meet one's daily requirements. Therefore it is very necessary that the eliminative faculty be quickened in one, and a right balance between receiving and giving, laying hold and letting go, be established" (MD 652-653).

When we love God we are willing to renounce the things in our consciousness and outer lives that do not belong to our spiritual natures.

Judas Iscariot represents life. In Judas we find the unredeemed life-forces that, unless handled spiritually, betray the Christ or spiritual self. The Christ life within us is pure and undefiled, but we, as individuals, can use this life energy any way we choose. Since people have used their lives destructively they have been deprived of their bodies. When we expend this life-force in the satisfaction of sense desires and pleasures we pervert it; devastation of mind and body then results. Judas was the treasurer for Jesus and His Apostles. He held the moneybag, and greed and covetousness ruled in him:

"The first step in our redeeming the Judas faculty is to assume a fearless attitude of mind, affirming our unity with the Spirit of purity. When we do this the Lord answers, 'Thou hast said,' and the redeeming, uplifting, transmuting forces are set into operation. When the Judas faculty reaches the spiritual standard of life it is known as Judah, whose office is praise and thanksgiving. Praise and thanksgiving call into activity greater expressions of spiritual substance and open larger avenues through which we may receive spiritual life. Praise radiates and gives glory to the latent powers of man" (MD 375).

When we are tempted to succumb to sense desires of an unworthy nature, it means that Judas is in control. In giving our attention to Christ as Jesus did, the greedy, selfish sense desires are eliminated (Judas is repentant and kills himself), thus giving the higher consciousness full reign to assert itself. To fill the place in their group that was left vacant by Judas, the Apostles chose Matthias, who represents the lifting up of the life faculty "that it may aid the individual in laying hold of his higher, spiritual attainments . . . through the power of his indwelling Christ" (MD 434).

"When man has brought his higher self into action he will see clearly the relation of spirit, soul, and body, in all places of their action" (TM 173).

Jesus taught that the goal of humankind is eternal life. Only those who have strengthened their faculties can appreciate the wonderful undeveloped possibilities in us; the spiritually minded person beholds them as all-potential.

CHAPTER VI

The New Law

Soon after the selection of the Twelve Apostles, Jesus delivered the immortal lessons that comprise the Sermon on the Mount. Even as the law that Moses received on Mount Sinai is the heart of Judaism, the Sermon on the Mount is the heart of Christianity. The Sermon is the new law; it is not meant to abrogate the revered Mosaic law but it is to teach us how this law may be fulfilled spiritually. The first law given to Moses, and which came from the heights of Sinai in the wilderness, was accompanied by thunder and lightning. The new law was enunciated from the summit of a grassy hill in Galilee, probably from an elevation known as the Horns of Hattin, as its two peaks resemble an Oriental saddle. Here a crowd gathered to see and hear the Master, whose words were spoken in quietness and in love. The "Thou shalt not" of the Ten Commandments is replaced by the words "Blessed are you" in the Sermon on the Mount. The Decalogue's stern delineation of right and wrong is mitigated in the Sermon to a compassionate appeal for righteous thinking and feeling. Moses stated the law; Jesus explained the way to obey it. We read in Matthew 5:1-12:

"Seeing the crowds, he [Jesus] went up on the mountain, and when he sat down his disciples came to him. And he opened his mouth and taught them, saying:
'Blessed are the poor in spirit, for theirs is the kingdom of heaven.' "

This is the first of the eight great statements called the Beatitudes. Each statement says that we shall be blessed when we attain certain attitudes of mind. The "poor in spirit" are people who relinquish their human concepts that they may learn from God. The intellect of humankind is marvelous indeed; yet, if we are to attain divine wisdom we must be humble (poor in spirit) toward Him and willing and eager to hear His words and follow them. This is the only way that our minds can expand Godward. As our minds develop, we come into the realization of the omnipresent good (the kingdom of heaven).

"Blessed are those who mourn, for they shall be comforted."

Trials and tribulations cause us to mourn. Yet it is true that ''man's extremity is God's opportunity,'' and when woes beset us we turn to Him and receive comfort.

''Blessed are the meek, for they shall inherit the earth.''

Meekness, spiritually considered, is an attitude of receptivity to the divine will. Jesus was meek when He said, ''Not as I will, but as thou wilt'' (Mt. 26:39). Meekness is a willingness to surrender to God and a confidence that His way is the better way. When the Christ expresses through us, we have power over external conditions (the earth).

''Blessed are those who hunger and thirst for righteousness, for they shall be satisfied.''

Righteousness is the right or spiritual use of mental, physical, and spiritual faculties, which are manifested as right action. When our desire to express the Christ is more powerful than our desire for personal gain or for personal power, we are hungering and thirsting after righteousness. The promise is that we shall be filled; that is, our desire shall be satisfied by divine love and divine life.

"Blessed are the merciful, for they shall obtain mercy."

The merciful are those who are kind in thought and in deed. On occasion we may feel impelled to help someone but we do it reluctantly. Such acts fall short of true mercy because thought and deed are at variance. We are only merciful when we realize that we are all brothers and sisters and that the good of one is the good of all, and act accordingly. We always receive mercy in proportion to our being merciful.

"Blessed are the pure in heart, for they shall see God."

Pure means unmixed, chaste, and free from defilement. A person whose heart is pure directs his whole attention to God, to good. Purity is one-pointed vision, the "single" eye. Impurity, in a spiritual sense, implies double vision, seeing good and evil. When the consciousness is so purified that we perceive only one Presence and one Power, we are, in reality, seeing God.

"Blessed are the peacemakers, for they shall be called sons of God."

The peacemakers are those who make peace outwardly because they have attained an inner peace. Since they are at peace with God they are also at peace with others, and they bring peace to all the conditions in which they are involved. We are sons and daughters of God, but our kinship is merely an inherent potentiality until we gain peace of mind and express it. Then we are His sons and daughters in actuality.

"Blessed are those who are persecuted for righteousness' sake, for theirs is the kingdom of heaven. Blessed are you when men revile you and persecute you and utter all kinds of evil against you falsely on my account. Rejoice and be glad, for your reward is great in heaven."

Those who are persecuted for righteousness' sake are ones who have spiritual ideals and yet encounter within themselves states of consciousness that oppose their ideals. These adverse states of consciousness belong to the race thought, much of which is still in each of us. These states are tenacious and unyielding and resist or persecute the ideals that we are endeavoring to maintain. Not only is there an inner conflict; there may be an outer one also: "men shall reproach you, and persecute you." When people do not understand our spiritual convictions they are apt to misjudge and condemn us. This beatitude promises that we shall be blessed if we maintain our ideals in the face of inner and outer persecution. We should actually rejoice and be glad, for our steadfastness will bring great spiritual advancement. This is our "reward in heaven," and heaven is the spiritual kingdom within all people.

From these basic statements that concern spiritual thought and feeling, Jesus proceeded with a more detailed account to show that the new law was to be put into operation through better understanding. He revealed our true identity by saying, "You are the salt of the earth" (Mt. 5:13) and "You are the light of the world" (Mt. 5:14). But He warned that the salt can lose its savor, and the light is often put under a bushel. This means that when we do not recognize our spiritual natures we lack the ability to express the power that is rightfully ours. Rather:

"Let your light so shine before men, that they

may see your good works and give glory to your Father who is in heaven'' (Mt. 5:16).

In the hands of the Jewish leaders of Jesus' day, the Mosaic law had become a routine of exaggerated scruples and formalism from which Spirit had been banished. Jesus clearly stated His position with reference to the law: ''Think not that I have come to abolish the law and the prophets; I have come not to abolish them but to fulfil them'' (Mt. 5:17). Nevertheless, our obedience to the law should exceed the righteousness of the scribes and Pharisees (Mt. 5:20); that is, it should be of the Spirit and not merely of the letter.

Jesus showed the difference between the manner in which the law was being obeyed and the requirements for its spiritual fulfillment. He enjoined forgiveness (''be reconciled to your brother''), nonresistance (''do not resist one who is evil''), morality in thought as well as in act (''every one who looks at a woman lustfully has already committed adultery with her in his heart''), a willingness to give more than is asked (''and if any one forces you to go one mile, go with him two miles''), and loving and praying for our enemies (''love your enemies and pray for those who persecute you"). "You, therefore, must be perfect, as your heavenly Father is perfect" (Mt. 5:24-48).

Alms should be given modestly, not with ostentation. We should not flaunt our piety before others, but display it for God only. "But when you pray, go into your room and shut the door and pray to your Father who is in secret; and your Father who sees in secret will reward you" (Mt. 6:6).

"Your room" signifies the inmost recesses of our being. It is sometimes referred to as the upper room or chamber, and the Psalmist poetically calls this inner sanctuary the "secret place of the Most High." It is here that we become aware of our oneness with God. As we enter the inner chamber by opening our consciousness to Him, our minds are closed to worldly considerations ("having shut the door"). Frequently the mind is so filled with outer interests it is difficult to release them and think of God. If persistent, we learn the secret of spiritual concentration and abide in the secret place. The prayer that we then make is in obedience to the rules of prayer, and we may rest in the promise that "your Father who sees in secret will reward you."

That His hearers might know how to pray

aright Jesus gave a model for all true prayer,
"The Lord's Prayer" (Mt. 6:9-13). It is all-
inclusive, encompassing the entire category of
human needs. Regardless of what words we use
in any prayer, they touch "The Lord's Prayer" at
some point. This mighty prayer, familiar to every
Christian, becomes a vital part of our prayer life
when our understanding of it deepens:

"Our Father" [the one life that all share]
"who art in heaven" [the spiritual realm],
"Hallowed be thy name" [holy is thy nature].

"Thy kingdom come" [the wholeness of thy
spirit be manifested],

"Thy will be done, On earth as it is in heav-
en" [thy perfect will come into expression on the
plane of manifestation, earth, as it is on the
spiritual heights]. "Give us this day our daily
bread" [all that is necessary to sustain life
spiritually, mentally, and physically];

"And forgive us our debts, As we also have
forgiven our debtors" [as we forgive others their
trespasses against us, we are forgiven];

"And lead us not into temptation, But deliver
us from evil." [This is perhaps the least understood portion of the prayer. God, who is perfect
good, could never bring or lead or leave us in
temptation, but it is undoubtedly true that we

are tested. This portion of the prayer asks that we may be delivered from the seeming powers of evil].

"For thine is the kingdom, and the power, and the glory, for ever" [is our recognition that God is the giver of all good and we acknowledge His supremacy].

"Amen" [so be it, is our acceptance in faith].

True prayers accumulate "treasures in heaven," i.e., a rich consciousness filled with faith and peace, "where neither moth nor rust consumes and where thieves do not break in and steal" (Mt. 6:20). Jesus pointed out that the "single" eye (seeing God only) brings wholeness to our lives and frees us from the darkness or limitation that comes from seeing good and evil.

"No one can serve two masters; for either he will hate the one and love the other, or he will be devoted to the one and despise the other. You cannot serve God and mammon" (Mt. 6:24).

Cares and anxieties as regards the material necessities of life should not divert our attention. Our first desire should be to serve God.

"Your heavenly Father knows that you need

them all. But seek first his kingdom and his righteousness, and all these things shall be yours as well'' (Mt. 6:32-33).

Jesus reminds us, ''How much more will your Father who is in heaven give good things to those who ask him!'' (Mt. 7:11) Therefore,

''Ask, and it will be given you; seek, and you will find; knock, and it will be opened to you. For every one who asks receives, and he who seeks finds, and to him who knocks it will be opened'' (Mt. 7:7-8).

The law of life gives perfect justice to all, and Jesus cautions us not to judge if we do not want to be judged. ''For with the judgment you pronounce you will be judged, and the measure you give will be the measure you get'' (Mt. 7:2). Why should we look for the faults of others when our own are close at hand and need correcting? ''You hypocrite, first take the log out of your own eye, and then you will see clearly to take the speck out of your brother's eye'' (Mt. 7:5).

Jesus instructed His listeners to enter in ''by the narrow gate.'' Narrow, indeed, is the gate and straight the way "that leads to life" (the more abundant life of Spirit), but "those who find it are few." Many people take the broad way that appears to be easier, but it "leads to destruction" (Mt. 7:13-14). It is given to each of us to choose the way we will take.

Jesus cautioned us against "false prophets"; that is, He warned us of certain religious teachers. These people promise much, but they have nothing to offer in the way of spiritual virtues. The corrupt tree can bring forth only evil fruit, but the good tree brings forth good fruit. If we do the "will of my Father" we produce good fruit, and "you will know them by their fruits."

Jesus ended the Sermon on the Mount by drawing a contrast between people who hear His sayings and disregard them and those who hear and do them. The former shall be likened unto a foolish man who builds his house on the sand. It cannot withstand the storm, and great is the fall thereof. The latter is "like a wise man who built his house upon the rock; and the rain fell, and the floods came, and the winds blew and beat upon that house, but it did not fall, because it had been founded on the rock" (Mt. 7:24-25).

When the Sermon on the Mount was ended,

Jesus returned to Capernaum and was met by a
Roman centurion who told Jesus that his faithful
servant was lying at the point of death. As Jesus
started toward the Roman officer's house, the
centurion said to Him, "Lord, I am not worthy
to have you come under my roof; but only say
the word, and my servant will be healed" (Mt.
8:8). Jesus was amazed and gratified by the
man's remarkable faith and said, "Go; be it
done for you as you have believed." And the
centurion's servant "was healed at that very moment" (Mt. 8:13).

The healing of the officer's servant is another
instance of "absent healing." The Roman centurion, though a man who had authority over
others, was humble before Jesus, whose greatness
he recognized and in whom he had faith. Our
humility and faith pave the way for spiritual
healing for ourselves and for our loved ones.

From Capernaum Jesus "went to a city called
Nain, and his disciples and a great crowd went
with him" (Lk. 7:11). As they entered the gate
to the town a sad procession met their eyes. It
was the funeral of a young man who was the only
son of a widow.

"And when the Lord saw her, he had compassion on her and said to her, 'Do not weep.' And he came and touched the bier, and the bearers stood still. And he said, 'Young man, I say to you, arise.' And the dead man sat up, and began to speak. And he gave him to his mother'' (Lk. 7:13-15).

This is the first account we have of Jesus' raising the dead. He understood that life is eternal. He proved that the body can be reanimated by the realization of the omnipresent life of Spirit. Jesus "touched the bier," meaning that He contacted the death belief and filled it with life. We constantly meet death in various forms: death of faith, death of hope, death of ambition, and so on. Can we raise these error thoughts to life? To do so should be the goal of all Christians. Should we falter along the way, we will find strength and comfort in the Master's words: "Come to me, all who labor and are heavy laden, and I will give you rest. Take my yoke upon you, and learn from me" (Mt. 11:28-29).

Busy days followed in the life of the Master. The Pharisees were curious about Him, and one of them, Simon by name, invited Jesus to dine with him. While they were sitting at table, a woman "who was a sinner" entered the room,

bringing with her an alabaster cruse of ointment. "And standing behind him at his feet,
weeping, she began to wet his feet with her tears,
and wiped them with the hair of her head, and
kissed his feet, and anointed them with the ointment" (Lk. 7:38). Simon thought that Jesus did
not know what kind of woman she was, since the
Master had allowed her to serve Him. It was the
custom of the Pharisees to draw aside their robes
when they met sinners. Then Jesus said to
Simon:

"A certain creditor had two debtors; one owed
five hundred denarii, and the other fifty. When
they could not pay, he forgave them both. Now
which of them will love him more?" (Lk.
7:41-42)

Simon replied that the one who owed the
most would feel the most loving. Then, pointing
to the woman, Jesus remarked that she had
treated Him with more love and respect than had
Simon.

" 'Therefore I tell you, her sins, which are
many, are forgiven, for she loved much; but he
who is forgiven little, loves little.' And he said to

her, 'Your sins are forgiven. . . . Your faith has saved you; go in peace' '' (Lk. 7:47-50).

This incident serves to remind us that our transgressions, even though they be of a serious nature, are forgiven if we love that which is spiritual and will turn from our wrongdoing to serve the Christ.

As Jesus journeyed through Galilee, stopping at many villages, Mary Magdalene, from whom He had formerly cast "seven devils" (mental obsessions); Joanna, the wife of Chuza, Herod's steward; Susanna, and many others ministered unto Him. The Scriptures do not record when or where the healing of Mary Magdalene took place. There is, however, no authority to connect her with either the sinful woman who washed the feet of Jesus at Simon's house or the woman taken in adultery. Tradition has associated Mary Magdalene with one of the two, and wrongly so. She is mentioned in the Gospels as a woman whom Jesus healed, and who later ministered to Him. She followed Him to the Cross and was the first to whom He made Himself known on the Resurrection morning.

The Pharisees were unable to understand Jesus' ability to heal physical and mental illnesses. They considered themselves more righteous than He, yet they could not perform healings similar to His. When word was relayed to them that Jesus had healed one possessed with a demon, blind and dumb, they said, "It is only by Beelzebul, the prince of demons, that this man casts out demons" (Mt. 12:24). Jesus replied that Satan cannot cast out Satan and that He healed "by the Spirit of God" (Mt. 12:28). Then He issued a stern warning:

"Therefore I tell you, every sin and blasphemy will be forgiven men, but the blasphemy against the Spirit will not be forgiven. And whoever says a word against the Son of man will be forgiven; but whoever speaks against the Holy Spirit will not be forgiven" (Mt. 12:31-32).

The "unforgivable sin," the speaking against the Holy Spirit, is our denial of the presence of God within us. When we think of ourselves as sick, poor, and miserable we are repudiating our true nature and denying the life and activity of the Holy Spirit in us. So long as we do this we cannot be forgiven. It is only by turning to God that we receive forgiveness. Whenever we will we may seek Him and be cleansed. But so long as we persistently turn from Him, deny Him, and maintain the errors of our ways, it is impossible for the forgiving love of our Father to be operative for us.

On one occasion as Jesus was teaching the multitudes, word was brought to Him that His mother and brothers wished to speak to Him:

"But he replied to the man who told him, 'Who is my mother, and who are my brothers?' And stretching out his hand toward his disciples, he said, 'Here are my mother and my brothers! For whoever does the will of my Father in heaven is my brother, and sister, and mother'" (Mt. 12:48-50).

Here Jesus seems to deny the bond of blood relationships and to recognize only spiritual kinship. This is a shortsighted view. Was He not giving us a greater conception of kindred? The ties of common belief, aspiration, and work are as strong as those of blood. Jesus' words give no ground for the assumption that He refused to see His mother and brothers or that He loved them less because He recognized a bond of kinship with His followers. He did not overlook His obligation to His mother; even on the Cross He made provision for her care. His remarks give us no justification for repudiating family or relatives, but they do imply that we should enlarge the scope of our love to include our friends and co-workers in the establishment of a spiritual world.

During the second year of His ministry Jesus gave His first great group of parables, though He had already used the parabolic form of teaching to some extent. A parable is a short, fictitious narrative based on a familiar experience and having an application to spiritual life. Invariably Jesus took an incident from everyday life to set forth a spiritual truth. The parable was a favorite Jewish mode of teaching, and Jesus imparted to it the richest and most perfect development. These great parables of Jesus included nine of the mysteries of the kingdom of heaven or the kingdom of God. In the gospel of Matthew, the phrase "kingdom of heaven" is used, whereas Mark and Luke use "kingdom of God." Both terms refer to the spiritual plane of our being, which is the storehouse of divine ideas. Charles Fillmore says:

"Jesus definitely located the kingdom of God (heaven) when He said, 'The kingdom of God is not coming with signs to be observed; nor will they say, "Lo, here it is!" or "There!" for behold, the kingdom of God is in the midst of you' (Lk. 17:20-21).

"In order to find this kingdom, we must become conscious of Divine Mind and its realm of divine ideas, and be willing to adjust our thoughts to the divine standard.

"Man adjusts his thought world to the kingdom of divine ideas through a process of denial by which he eliminates from consciousness all inharmonious ideas, and through affirmations of Truth by which he establishes himself in harmony with divine ideas.

"Heaven is not confined to man's consciousness. It is everywhere present. When man's mind and body are in harmonious relation to divine ideas, his true thoughts flow into the realm of manifestation and bring forth the kingdom in the earth 'as in heaven' " (MD 387-388).

To realize the kingdom within is the highest ideal we can set for ourselves. Each of the following parables gives a practical lesson on how to attain the consciousness of this inner kingdom.

"And the whole crowd stood on the beach" (Mt. 13:2) as Jesus spoke various parables to them from a boat that was kept for Him on the Sea of Galilee for that purpose.

Parable of the Sower

(Mt. 13:3-9, 18-23)

"A sower went out to sow." The sower is the indwelling Christ who is always speaking the word of Truth to us (sowing the seed). Four types of hearers are described. The first hears the word but is so lacking in spiritual understanding that sense consciousness quickly obliterates it. The seeds "fell along the path, and the birds came and devoured them." The second hears the word, receives it gladly, and remembers it for a time. However, this person has only a superficial knowledge of Truth, and when trials come thrusts the word aside. This hearer's mind is like the "rocky ground, where they had not much soil." The sprouting seed, not having enough roots, is scorched by the sun's rays. The third hears the word, and this person's mind is like thorny ground. He or she is obsessed with a sense of burden ("the cares of the world") and absorbed in the pursuit of wealth ("the delight in riches"). These are thorns that choke the seed and keep it from growing. The fourth hearer, as a result of study of spiritual things and love for God, has a receptive mind. This represents the "good soil" that produces an abundant harvest. Each of us has the power to choose the kind of consciousness that we will have, and the outcome of our hearing the word will either be indifferent or beneficial, according to the way in which we receive it. The seed falls into our mind and responds to our consciousness.

Parable of the Growing Seed

(Mk. 4:26-29)

In this parable Jesus teaches that our consciousness develops spiritually in the same mysterious way that seeds do when planted in the ground. An idea that is sown in the mind will grow if it receives the nourishment and the encouragement it requires. Understanding, faith, persistence, and application allow divine ideas to unfold in an orderly manner: "First the blade, then the ear, then the full grain in the ear." We do not reap a harvest as soon as the seed is sown; neither do we receive the entire good we desire immediately after we plant divine ideas in our consciousness. Our spiritual development, like physical development, is progressive, and if we will be patient and faithful, we shall surely come to the time of rich fulfillment.

Parable of the Tares (Weeds)

(Mt. 13:24-30, 36-43)

This parable has a particularly practical lesson for us. It explains why there is a mixture of good and evil in consciousness, even though our desire is for good only. Through study and earnest prayer we deliberately plant constructive thoughts (wheat), yet we are often dismayed when we find destructive thoughts (tares) still lodging in our minds. The tares are sown by the sense consciousness (enemy) at times when we are not on the alert spiritually ("while men were sleeping"). Our first impulse is to uproot the tares immediately, that is, forcibly to dismiss the destructive thoughts. This action would be unwise. It is better to "let both grow together until the harvest." It would be difficult to cleanse our minds thoroughly in the early stages of our spiritual development. If we attempted to do this, we might destroy much that is good along with the evil. When we have attained sufficient spiritual understanding (time of harvest), a separation can safely be made and the good ideas preserved as the evil beliefs are cast out.

Parable of the Mustard Seed

(Mt. 13:31-32)

How does spiritual realization (the kingdom) begin? Like all great accomplishments, it starts with an idea. An initial divine idea is small amidst the multitude of other thoughts in the mind. It is like a tiny mustard seed sown in a field. Yet, an idea born of Spirit has in it tremendous life and power. It will grow until it becomes as strong and sturdy as a tree and will serve as a lodging place for additional spiritual ideas ("the birds of the air").

Parable of the Leaven

(Mt. 13:33)

We must take deliberate action if we would come into a higher realization of Truth. Even as it is necessary to put leaven into bread if it is to be fit to eat, so must we put the word of Truth into the conditions of our lives if we are to express the good. Like the action of the leaven, our word does its work invisibly and silently. At first, we may be tempted to think that no progress is being made, but just as surely as the leaven caused the three measures of meal to rise, even so our word, spoken in faith, lifts our understanding to loftier heights. In due time, we become aware that a substantial and beneficial change has taken place and we realize that we have attained a great growth in consciousness.

Parable of the Hidden Treasure

(Mt. 13:44)

The teaching here is that we may discover Truth quite unexpectedly, just as a man digging in a field may, seemingly by chance, unearth a hidden treasure. For a time we keep this precious secret to ourselves and hide it in our hearts. Eventually, however, we realize that if we are to have the benefit of God's good we must pay a price for it. The cost is our surrender to Him in time, devotion, and obedience ("sells all that he has"). Then the treasure is ours to be used to make life fuller and richer in every way.

Parable of the Pearl of Great Price

(Mt. 13:45-46)

There is a marked similarity between this parable and the preceding one. In both there is the discovery that Truth is the great good (treasure and pearl). Sometimes this realization comes unexpectedly, as in the parable of the hidden treasure, although in this case it is the result of unconscious desire. In the parable of the great pearl we are likened to the merchant who is definitely seeking a better thing. Our desire for it has become wholly conscious, and we are persistent in our search. We have already accumulated much that is worthwhile (the merchant had

smaller gems) but we are not satisfied, for we
know that there is yet something greater to be acquired. Seeking, we shall surely find, and we
eventually come to understand that God is the
ultimate good. We then have located our great
pearl. We realize our oneness with God. Joyously
we sever our attachment to the lesser blessings
that we have demonstrated, knowing that all our
needs, both inner and outer, are provided for.

Parable of the Net

(Mt. 13:47-51)

We live in a great sea of universal life. Our
minds accumulate every kind of thought, like a
net that has been "thrown into the sea and gathered fish of every kind." When we come into an
understanding of Truth we have the discernment
to separate good ideas from limited beliefs. The
ideas that increase our spiritual stature are
carefully preserved, and the erroneous concepts
that breed various kinds of trouble are cast away.
The phrase "close of the age" that is used in this
parable and in the parable of the tares does not
mean a physical dissolution of the earth; it refers

to the end of some phase of our own experience. A drastic change in our affairs marks the end of one age and the beginning of another. If we will ask for divine guidance at such a time, our spiritual ideas (angels) will overcome the vicious and destructive thoughts ("throw them into the furnace of fire"). Yet, these negative states of mind that belong to the race consciousness do not relinquish their hold on us without protest ("there men will weep and gnash their teeth"), and our salvation lies in our steadfastness in Truth. When Jesus had finished the parable of the net He inquired of His hearers, "Have you understood all this?" Their affirmative answer brought forth His concluding parable:

Parable of the Householder

(Mt. 13:52)

As we hear, comprehend, and obey the word of Truth we become a disciple in "the kingdom of heaven" and are like a householder "who brings out of his treasure what is new and what is old." Our treasure consists of all that goes to make up our spiritual consciousness. Part of it has been accumulated in the past. Every good thought and deed has made a contribution to righteousness, and this (the old) we retain. But spiritual unfoldment has no ending, and as we listen to the Christ in us and understand His word, realization on realization is added (the new.)

"And when Jesus had finished these parables, he went away from there" (Mt. 13:53). Deciding to cross the Sea of Galilee, Jesus and His Apostles entered a boat, and when they had set sail Jesus fell asleep. After a time a storm arose. The waves washed into the boat, and it began to fill with water. The Apostles were greatly frightened and awoke Jesus, saying, "Teacher, do you not care if we perish?" (Mk. 4:38).

"And he awoke and rebuked the wind, and said to the sea, 'Peace! Be still!' And the wind ceased, and there was a great calm. He said to them, 'Why are you afraid? Have you no faith?' " (Mk. 4:39-40)

This miracle shows the power that spiritual man has even over the elements. The Apostles represent the human consciousness that is terrified by the storm. The storm symbolizes any sort of threatening occurrence in life. These men called to Jesus for help. In times of stress we call on the Christ spirit within us. When the indwelling Christ is aroused by our call, He takes charge, and the storm subsides. Jesus then asked a question that we often ask ourselves, "Why are you afraid? Have you no faith?" We have seen the exercise of spiritual power; we know that Truth works; yet when storms of various kinds arise, we are fearful and our faith diminishes. If we can remember to turn quickly to the Christ (awaken Jesus), He will assume command and adjust matters. Then we shall be amazed at the might of Spirit—"Who then is this, that even wind and sea obey him?" (Mk. 4:41) Once more we will view with awe and reverence the marvelous works of the Son of God.

Up to this time, Jesus' ministry had been confined almost entirely to Judea and Galilee. After He crossed the Sea of Galilee He entered that section of country known as the Decapolis, an area made up of ten Greek cities, whose inhabitants were mostly Gentiles. This was Jesus' first journey to non-Jewish territory. On their arrival Jesus and His companions were met by a man who is referred to as the Gerasene demoniac. Jesus had healed several such afflicted people before, and He said, ''Come out of the man, you unclean spirit!'' (Mk. 5:8)

In those days it was the common belief that an insane person was possessed of demons with lives and intelligence of their own, demons who resisted all efforts to drive them from their abode in a person. The Bible records that the demons mentioned in this incident recognized the power of Jesus which could cast them out, and they implored Him to send them into a herd of swine grazing on the mountainside. ''So he gave them leave. And the unclean spirits came out, and entered the swine; and the herd, numbering about two thousand, rushed down the steep bank into the sea, and were drowned in the sea'' (Mk. 5:13).

This incident about the demoniac is perhaps one of the most obscure passages in the Bible, and any attempt to interpret it literally is well nigh impossible. *The Abingdon Bible Commentary* (page 1006) gives a brief explanation:

''It would seem that Jesus on this first visit of His to the Decapolis . . . met a man suffering from the delusion that he was possessed of a legion of evil spirits. After some conversation with him Jesus was able to deliver him from the delusion and restore him to mental health.''

But what is the spiritual significance of the event? With regard to demons Charles Fillmore states:

"Demons, or evil spirits, are conditions of mind, or states of consciousness, that have been developed because the creative power of man has been used in an unwise or an ignorant way. . . . The mind builds states of consciousness that become established in brain and body. Both good and evil are found in the unregenerate man, but in the new birth evil and all its works must be cast out. The work of every overcomer is to cast out of himself the demons of sin and evil, through the power and dominion of his indwelling Christ' (MD 170).

Adverse states of consciousness (demons) are tenacious and do not relinquish their hold easily. When their rule is threatened by our determined efforts to be rid of them, they seek other habitats or places of residence in consciousness. For example, we may have allowed excessive fears as regards some bodily condition to take root in our minds. When these fears are about to be "cast out'' as a result of prayer, they are quite likely to seek expression in some other circumstances of life. Swine are unclean animals and represent sensuous, impure thoughts. In this healing the demons left the man at the command of Jesus and entered the swine. This means that obsessions that are dislodged at one point in consciousness find temporary refuge in some other phase of the carnal nature. As the herd rushed into the sea and perished, so evil is ultimately destroyed if we will be faithful in focusing our thought energy on the indwelling Christ and claim union with Him.

CHAPTER VII

Clouds of Opposition

(Second Year)

After Jesus visited the territory of the Gera-
senes He returned to His headquarters in Capernaum, where He was met by Jairus, a ruler of the
synagogue. Jairus beseeched Jesus to come to his
home to heal his young daughter, who was criti-
cally ill. Jesus immediately responded, but the
great crowds that followed Him slowed His progress.

"And there was a woman who had had a flow
of blood for twelve years, and who had suffered
much under many physicians, and had spent all
that she had, and was no better but rather grew
worse. She had heard the reports about Jesus,
and came up behind him in the crowd and
touched his garment. For she said, 'If I touch
even his garments, I shall be made well.' And
immediately the hemorrhage ceased; and she felt
in her body that she was healed of her disease''
(Mk. 5:25-29).

This incident is one of the great lessons on

faith. The woman had been ill for a long time, yet she had not given up hope of regaining her health. When she heard of the remarkable cures that Jesus had effected, she made a determined effort to reach Him by pushing through the crowd. Her faith was so strong that she believed she would recover, even if she only touched the hem of His garment.

Healing comes when we make contact with the Christ, whom Jesus represents. We need to come boldly before the throne of grace and push through the "crowd"—our own destructive thoughts and feelings—that separates us from our Christ self. Our part is to be persistent in making our way through them. Jesus said that it was the woman's faith which brought about her healing, and faith also brings healing to us. If we believe that it is God's will for us to be well we will not let anything keep us from contacting the Christ and receiving wholeness from Him.

While Jesus was speaking to the woman who had touched His garment, word was brought to Jairus that his daughter had died and that there was no need for Jesus to come.

"But Jesus on hearing this answered him, 'Do not fear; only believe, and she shall be well.'

And when he came to the house, he permitted no one to enter with him, except Peter and John and James, and the father and mother of the child. And all were weeping and bewailing her; but he said, 'Do not weep; for she is not dead but sleeping.' And they laughed at him, knowing that she was dead. But taking her by the hand he called, saying, 'Child, arise.' And her spirit returned, and she got up at once; and he directed that something should be given her to eat'' (Lk. 8:50-55).

This was the second instance where Jesus raised a dead person, and it is recorded in sufficient detail for us to understand the steps that He took in performing the miracle. When He entered the home He shut out the multitude, but took Peter (faith), James (judgment), John (love), and the parents with Him. The three statements Jesus made contain the secret of a quickening from death to life. First, He said to the child's father, ''Do not fear; only believe, and she shall be well.'' Fear must be dismissed from consciousness and replaced with a steadfast faith. Second, He denied the reality of death: ''She is not dead but sleeping.'' The life of God that gives animation to the body always exists.

Then He spoke directly to the Christ life within the child and said to her, "Child, arise." The word spoken in faith brings about a restoration.

As Jesus departed from the home of Jairus, two blind men followed Him and begged to be healed. He asked, "Do you believe that I am able to do this?" When they replied in the affirmative, He touched their eyes, and they were opened.

"And Jesus sternly charged them, 'See that no one knows it' " (Mt. 9:30).

On several occasions Jesus told persons whom He had healed not to speak about their healings. There is a definite reason for this. In telling of a spiritual healing, a person speaks also of the limitation that has been overcome, and it is easy for the mind to slip back into the consciousness of the limitation. This is likely to bring about a return of the troublesome condition. It is best to give thanks for the healing and then give full attention to right living in the present. A person is justified in telling of a demonstration only when his doing so will serve to inspire another's faith.

Jesus then returned to Nazareth. He had not been back to His hometown since He had spoken

in the synagogue there at the beginning of His
Galilean ministry, at which time He had aroused
the enmity of the Jewish leaders. This was before
His fame had become so widespread. On this
second visit these leaders still resented Him. Was
He not simply a carpenter, the son of Mary,
whose family resided among them?

"And Jesus said to them, 'A prophet is not
without honor, except in his own country, and
among his own kin, and in his own house.' And
he could do no mighty work there, except that
he laid his hands upon a few sick people and
healed them. And he marveled because of their
unbelief" (Mk. 6:4-6).

It is sometimes difficult to believe that what
is so close to us has any outstanding value.
"Distance lends enchantment" is a true adage.
We are loath to acknowledge the Christ within,
for we seem to be such commonplace persons.
Because we do not fully believe in the mighty
power that is "closer . . . than breathing," we
too often close the door to the good that Spirit
would gladly bestow. Jesus was astonished that
the people whom He knew intimately could not
accept Him. However, others did accept Him,

and great crowds followed Him wherever He went. Yet the friends whom He longed to help had no faith in Him, and He was powerless to help them. Without our faith and willingness to receive, the Christ spirit cannot move through us to bring blessings.

This second rebuff separated Jesus from the village of His childhood, and He never returned to Nazareth again. Instead, He went throughout the cities and towns of Galilee, "teaching in their synagogues and preaching the gospel of the kingdom, and healing every disease and every infirmity" (Mt. 9:35).

During His third tour of Galilee, Jesus was moved with compassion when He saw the multitudes that followed Him. They reminded Him of sheep without a shepherd, of a harvest that is ripe but unreaped for lack of laborers. He bade His Apostles pray to the Lord of the harvest that He would send forth laborers into His fields. Each of us should pray that we may be worthy to be used by the Father in serving Him and bringing His abundant good into manifestation.

Immediately after He had traversed the whole of Galilee, Jesus sent His Apostles "to the lost sheep of the house of Israel." He sent them two by two, to confirm His teaching and to heal in

His name:

"And preach as you go, saying, 'The kingdom of heaven is at hand.' Heal the sick, raise the dead, cleanse lepers, cast out demons. You received without paying, give without pay" (Mt. 10:7-8).

This is the work of the Christian disciple today. If we are to enter into the Christ consciousness, we must begin now to do His work in our own consciousness. Our preaching should concern the immediacy of the kingdom; that is, we should tell ourselves over and over again that God is good and that God is here. We should heal the sick thoughts, cleanse the leprous or unclean emotions, and cast out the mean and corrupt states of mind. We have received freely from God, who gave us of Himself. We should give freely of our spiritual resources to the unredeemed forces of our being.

As we are lifted up in consciousness, the time comes when we are also to serve outwardly. But as we go forth in His name,

"Take no gold, nor silver, nor copper in your belts, no bag for your journey, nor two tunics, nor sandals, nor a staff; for the laborer deserves his food'' (Mt. 10:9-10).

Material things do not give us the power to accomplish; yet a firm and steadfast consciousness coupled with a burning desire to do His work does supply this power. We do not need gold so much as we need ideas. Our physical needs will be provided as we serve Him faithfully.

''Behold, I send you out as sheep in the midst of wolves; so be wise as serpents and innocent as doves. Beware of men; for they will deliver you up to councils, and flog you in their synagogues, and you will be dragged before governors and kings for my sake, to bear testimony before them and the Gentiles. When they deliver you up, do not be anxious how you are to speak or what you are to say; for what you are to say will be given to you in that hour; for it is not you who speak, but the Spirit of your Father speaking through you'' (Mt. 10:16-20).

The path of spiritual service, whether in the home, the business world, or the ministry, has its hazards, as does every other meritorious endeavor. Jesus did not say that the way is easy, but

He did say that it is worthwhile and that we should not fear malicious power in the outer world. We will know what to say when we are attacked or persecuted for our convictions, because the Father whom we are serving will speak through us. There may be times when we are delivered up to our enemies, outer forces that seem mightier than we are, but we have Jesus' assurance of protection.

"Do not think that I have come to bring peace on earth; I have not come to bring peace, but a sword. For I have come to set a man against his father, and a daughter against her mother, and a daughter-in-law against her mother-in-law; and a man's foes will be those of his own household. . . . And he who does not take his cross and follow me is not worthy of me. He who finds his life will lose it, and he who loses his life for my sake will find it" (Mt. 10:34-39).

Jesus' words as regards peace will likely startle us when we first read them. Was He not the Prince of Peace? We should take into consideration that there are two kinds of peace: one is destructive, and the other is constructive. Peace at any price, which means the surrender of one's highest beliefs to appease another, is destructive. Jesus did not advocate this sort of peace. Peace that results from our sense of oneness with God is constructive, and Jesus referred to this when He said, "Peace I leave with you; my peace I give to you; not as the world gives do I give to you. Let not your hearts be troubled, neither let them be afraid" (Jn. 14:27). Such is an inward peace, the peace of God. It can function in the very midst of turmoil.

Jesus' declaration that He came not to bring peace but a sword was made to His intimate friends, the Apostles, who were going out to do His works. He warned them not to compromise His teachings for the sake of popularity. His words were like a sword that would cut through erroneous beliefs, and His Apostles would not be liked.

We must be prepared for a conflict between old human concepts and new spiritual ideas. The latter are higher than beliefs that are entertained by the sense mind, and for a time the clash of the two causes an agitation in consciousness. This is a part of our spiritual progress, and we should not fear it. Truth is sharp like a sword and cuts through the states of mind that we no longer desire and know that we do not need.

The restricting thoughts that are resident in the personal consciousness are our only enemies, for "a man's foes will be those of his own household." These thoughts must be crossed out if we are to be worthy of our high calling, which is to follow Him. The person who makes material things the aim and object of his existence, or who finds a full life in worldly pursuits, loses his capacity for spiritual expression, which is his real life. On the other hand, the person who is willing to lose outer gain for the attainment of spiritual understanding and service ("loses his life for my sake") will enjoy the more abundant life of Spirit.

During the absence of the Apostles on their missionary tour, Jesus continued His work. Herod Antipas, the ruler of Galilee, heard reports of what Jesus was doing and was exceedingly fearful. Herod had considered John a religious fanatic, and he considered Jesus of the same caliber. "This is John the Baptist, he has been raised from the dead" (Mt. 14:2), Herod exclaimed, and he sought to see Jesus. But Jesus, who had heard of the cruel and senseless slaying of John the Baptist, departed from Galilee as soon as the Apostles returned. "Come away by yourselves to a lonely place, and rest a while"

(Mk. 6:31). This was Jesus' invitation to them. However, many persons, seeing them leave, followed Jesus to the east coast of the Sea of Galilee. He had compassion on them and instead of resting, He taught the multitude all day.

The crowd of five thousand listened eagerly. When night began to fall the Apostles suggested that Jesus send them into the nearby villages to find food. "For we are here in a lonely place" they said (Lk. 9:12). Instead, Jesus commanded the Apostles to feed the multitude, which seemed impossible to them, as they could find only five loaves and two fish:

"And taking the five loaves and the two fish he looked up to heaven, and blessed and broke them, and gave them to the disciples to set before the crowd. And all ate and were satisfied. And they took up what was left over, twelve baskets of broken pieces" (Lk. 9:16-17).

This is a very spectacular miracle, and many efforts have been made by sincere Christians to explain it in terms of human possibility. Some have advanced the theory that the people who heard Jesus that day were so filled with spiritual nourishment that they felt no need for food.

Others have said that many of His hearers had food with them and shared it with others. Unity accepts the miracle literally, for it is clear evidence of the ability of spiritual man (Jesus Christ) to mold the ever-present substance and bring it into manifestation. Charles Fillmore states:

"The origin or source of all substance is the idea of substance. It is purely spiritual and can be apprehended only by the mind. It is never visible to the eye, nor can it be sensed by man through any of the bodily faculties. . . .

"When the mind has centered its attention on this idea of substance long enough and strongly enough, it generates the consciousness of substance, and through the powers of the various faculties of the mind in right relation it can form visible substance. Jesus in this way brought into visibility the loaves and fishes to feed the five thousand" (MJ 73-74).

The details that are given on this miracle of feeding the multitude contain a practical and helpful lesson in demonstration for us. The Apostles and the crowd represent the human way of viewing things. To them there was no possibility of finding food for the multitude on the arid plain where they were. Oftentimes we find ourselves in conditions that seem just as barren, but we can train ourselves to remember that even in such conditions there is much that is available, if only we know how to bring it forth. Here is a concise formula for the demonstration of substance. Jesus looked to heaven by fixing His attention on spiritual substance, the source of abundance. He did not think about lack. He thought about abundance, and then thanked God for the supply at hand. To praise our Lord and to give thanks for what we have is the surest way to increase our supply. If we have a little health or a little supply, we can add to it by praise and thanksgiving. Gratitude opens our consciousness to receive more. A supply of good is always available, for God is omnipresent. Jesus broke the five loaves and the two fish and gave the pieces to the Apostles to distribute to the multitude. This shows that we are to use what we have, though it be but a small amount. If we use what we have wisely, we make room for more. If muscles are not exercised they become flabby. If we have only a small amount of money and hoard it, we shut off the possibilities of gaining more. The law is that we must give, and we shall then receive. There is never a lack of good. There is only a lack of realization on our part that God's limitless substance is available to His children.

The miracle of the loaves and fish so impressed the people that they wanted to make Jesus a king (Jn. 6:14-15). Such was not His desire. Perceiving their intention, He withdrew to a mountain to pray, having first instructed the Apostles to go on ahead of Him to Capernaum.

Entering their boat, the Apostles started across the Sea of Galilee. Soon a storm arose. When it was at the height of its fury, they saw a figure walking toward them on the water. They cried out in fear, thinking that it was an apparition. Then a voice sounded through the darkness, saying, "Take heart, it is I; have no fear" (Mt. 14:27), and they recognized it as the voice of their beloved Master.

"And Peter answered him, 'Lord, if it is you, bid me come to you on the water.' He said, 'Come.' So Peter got out of the boat and walked on the water and came to Jesus; but when he saw the wind, he was afraid, and beginning to sink he cried out, 'Lord, save me.' Jesus immediately reached out his hand and caught him, saying to him, 'O man of little faith, why did you doubt?' '' (Mt. 14:28-31)

Peter represents faith, and faith dares to do that which seems impossible. Believing that he could also walk on the water at Jesus' command, Peter started toward the Master. However, before he reached Jesus his attention was distracted by the storm and he became fearful. As soon as fear entered his consciousness, Peter began to sink. There are times when we have the faith to begin projects, yet when obstacles arise we falter. When we begin to sink, will we remember to do what Peter did? He called to Jesus, and Jesus immediately held out His hand to the wavering apostle. Perhaps from this very experience, Peter learned the lesson that enabled him to say to the crowd on the Day of Pentecost, "And it shall be that whoever calls on the name of the Lord shall be saved" (Acts 2:21).

The people who had eaten the loaves and fish that Jesus had multiplied and who wanted to make Him king lost Him overnight, but they finally located Him the next morning in Capernaum. Jesus knew that they followed Him not for the spiritual teaching He gave but because they "ate of the loaves and were filled." He admonished them, "Do not labor for the food which perishes, but for the food which endures to eternal life, which the Son of man will give to you; for on him has God the Father set his seal" (Jn. 6:27).

This is the beginning of Jesus' great teaching that is known as the Discourse on the Bread of Life and is recorded in the sixth chapter of John. The people wanted to know how they might do the "works of God," and Jesus replied, "This is the work of God, that you believe in him whom he has sent" (Jn. 6:29). We are to believe in the indwelling Christ whom God has given us. The people then requested a sign from Him that they might believe. They said their ancestors had eaten the bread from heaven, the manna that fell when Moses prayed. Could not Jesus then give them a similar sign? Jesus replied, "Truly, truly, I say to you, it was not Moses who gave you the bread from heaven; my Father gives you the true bread from heaven" (Jn. 6:32). They asked for this bread, and Jesus said:

"I am the bread of life; he who comes to me shall not hunger, and he who believes in me shall never thirst. But I said to you that you have seen me and yet do not believe. All that the

Father gives me will come to me; and him who comes to me I will not cast out. For I have come down from heaven, not to do my own will, but the will of him who sent me; and this is the will of him who sent me, that I should lose nothing of all that he has given me, but raise it up at the last day. For this is the will of my Father, that every one who sees the Son and believes in him should have eternal life'' (Jn. 6:35-40).

The spirit of God in us, the Christ, is our source of nourishment, our bread of life. When we believe in and trust the Christ self as it is revealed to us, we attain an awareness of the eternal life which is of God. Charles Fillmore states:

''All shall attain who believe or have faith in the spiritual source of life. Whoever comes to this Christ realm in the heavens all about us will be moved by its will, which is the will of the Father. There will be no loss, no failure in this realm, and whoever enters into the Mind of Spirit will have poured out to him its life essence and be wholly raised up from material conditions when arriving at the 'last day' (the last degree of understanding)'' (MJ 74-75).

Jesus' words on the true bread sounded very strange to the listening Jews. They were shocked and began to take exception to what He said. They questioned, as others also had questioned: Was not this man the son of Joseph, and had they not known His parents? How could He say that He came down out of heaven? Jesus warned:

"Truly, truly, I say to you, he who believes has eternal life. I am the bread of life. Your fathers ate the manna in the wilderness, and they died. This is the bread which comes down from heaven, that a man may eat of it and not die. I am the living bread which came down from heaven; if any one eats of this bread, he will live for ever; and the bread which I shall give for the life of the world is my flesh" (Jn. 6:47-51).

The Jews could not comprehend how Jesus could give them His flesh to eat. But He insisted: "Unless you eat the flesh of the Son of man and drink his blood, you have no life in you . . . . For my flesh is food indeed, and my blood is drink indeed. He who eats my flesh and drinks my blood abides in me, and I in him" (Jn. 6:53-56). Jesus was here foreshadowing the teaching that He was to give later at the Last

Supper when He instituted what we now call the Communion. The body (flesh) and blood of Jesus represent the substance and life of Christ. When our minds appropriate this idea of divine substance and divine life, we symbolically are eating His flesh and drinking His blood.

To many who had followed Jesus up to this time, His words were a "hard saying." They could not believe, and "walked no more with him."

"Many people start out to walk in the light of Spirit, to unfold Truth, but they become entangled in their own misgivings and disbelief and therefore return to their old limited way of life" (MJ 76-77).

We can imagine how Jesus must have felt when He turned to the Twelve and asked, "Do you also wish to go away?" Peter replied: "Lord, to whom shall we go? You have the words of eternal life; and we have believed, and have come to know, that you are the Holy One of God" (Jn. 6:68-69). Staunch and courageous words these! It is sometimes difficult for us to understand and believe the deep things that are revealed by Spirit. Yet, when faith (Peter) has been quickened in consciousness, we know that Spirit is the only one to whom we can turn; there is no other source that can give us the words of eternal life. Such occasions are testing times for those of us who are on the spiritual path. If we affirm our faith in Christ, we gain strength, and the seeming mysteries are clarified.

This particular teaching utterly crushed the hopes of persons who looked to Jesus as a political Messiah to whose cause they could rally. His words were abhorrent to the orthodox Jews. Many whom He had healed and helped still loved Him even though they did not understand, but these constituted a small minority. From this time Jesus' cause in Galilee seemed doomed.

Shortly after Jesus gave His Discourse on the Bread of Life, another incident occurred that deepened the rift between Him and the Jews. Some scribes and Pharisees from Jerusalem had observed that Jesus' Apostles ate without washing their hands in the prescribed manner. They were violating the oral tradition, and its regulations were extremely elaborate and numerous. Before every meal and at every return from market a Jew was commanded to wash. If there were no water at hand, he was obliged to go at least four miles to search for it. In addition, there were rules for the washing of all cups, banquet couches, and brazen vessels, and no less than twenty-six prayers accompanied these tasks. They asked, "Why do your disciples transgress the tradition of the elders?" (Mt. 15:2) Instead of answering, Jesus put a question to them: "And why do you transgress the commandment of God for the sake of your tradition?" (Mt. 15:3) He reminded them that God commands a man to honor his father and mother, yet the scribes made a rule that if a person gave into the Temple treasury the sum that was intended for his parents, he did not have to support them. The scribes twisted a good law for their own benefit, yet they assumed a self-righteous attitude that concerned the breaking of a tradition that had no real value.

"And he [Jesus] called the people to him and said to them, 'Hear and understand: not what goes into the mouth defiles a man, but what comes out of the mouth, this defiles a man'" (Mt. 15:10-11).

It is not the outer observance of religious forms that is of importance, but what is in the heart of a person. If evil is in the heart, the mouth speaks it, and that which comes out of the heart is what defiles a man. To hide their corruptness, the Jewish leaders put emphasis on trifling details. Jesus knew that the leadership they furnished would lead the people to ruin. He said, "They are blind guides. And if a blind man leads a blind man, both will fall into a pit" (Mt. 15:14).

Throughout the second year of His ministry, Jesus had preached and healed, principally in Galilee, moving among the people and seizing every opportunity to instruct and help them. His words and great works attracted widespread attention, and for a time it seemed that the Galileans would follow Him. By the end of the year, however, it became evident that this was not to be. The Pharisees had become increasingly resentful of Jesus, and they had great influence over the masses. Jesus had antagonized the Pharisees by dishonoring many things they had been taught to regard as sacred. Perhaps they should be pitied more than blamed, for they were spiritually blind. Their own hard-and-fast rules closed their eyes to any improvements in religion, and they considered Jesus to be a deceiver of the people. At first He had attempted to ex-

plain His ideas, but the Pharisees were uncon-
vinced. When He continued His ministry in
spite of their objections, they grew to hate Him.
They did everything they could to turn the people against Him, and when the tide of His popularity began to wane at the end of His second
year of ministry, they took advantage of this and
attacked Him more viciously.

The conflict between Jesus and the Pharisees
represents the inevitable clash between the sense
man and the spiritual consciousness:

"For my thoughts are not your thoughts, neither are your ways my ways, says the Lord. For as
the heavens are higher than the earth, so are my
ways higher than your ways and my thoughts
than your thoughts" (Is. 55:8-9).

CHAPTER VIII

Crucifixion and Resurrection Foretold

(Third Year)

To all appearances the Pharisees had gained
the upper hand temporarily. Perceiving that little could be accomplished in Galilee, Jesus and
His Apostles journeyed to Tyre and Sidon, cities
of Phoenicia.

It was during Jesus' sojourn in Phoenicia that
the healing of the daughter of a Canaanite
woman took place (Mt. 15:21-28). The mother
was a Gentile, and when she asked Jesus for
help, He replied, "I was sent only to the lost
sheep of the house of Israel" (Mt. 15:24). Literally, His words mean that, as a Jew, He felt
that His ministry should be to His own race. It
was not until after the Resurrection that He commanded the Apostles, "Go into all the world
and preach the gospel to the whole creation"
(Mk. 16:15). The spiritual significance of Jesus'
words to the Gentile woman is that Gentiles represent the worldly mind, but Jews (Children of
Israel) represent the mind that is turned toward
God. Only persons who have some love for and

171

understanding of Truth can receive spiritual enlightenment. However, the mother persisted in
her plea, showing that faith was awakening in
her. To Jesus' objection, "It is not fair to take
the children's bread and throw it to the dogs,"
which means that it is wise to use care in sharing
spiritual things with those still in the depths of
mortal consciousness, the woman replied, "Yes,
Lord, yet even the dogs eat the crumbs that fall
from their masters' table." Though she knew
she was unworthy, she believed that Jesus would
help her. Her humility and faith aroused Jesus'
compassion, and He commended her, saying,
" 'O woman, great is your faith! Be it done for
you as you desire.' And her daughter was healed
instantly." Even though we may still be functioning largely on the plane of mortal thought, a
humble faith in God enables us to receive His
good.

From Phoenicia Jesus and His Apostles went
again to the Decapolis, east of the Jordan River.
On their arrival a deaf and dumb man was
brought to Jesus.

"And taking him aside from the multitude
privately, he put his fingers into his ears, and he
spat and touched his tongue; and looking up to

heaven, he sighed, and said to him, 'Eph-phatha,' that is, 'Be opened.' And his ears were opened, his tongue was released, and he spoke plainly'' (Mk. 7:33-35).

This healing is one of the few instances in which Jesus combined physical action with speaking the word, and it serves as a reminder to us that though we are receiving physical help, we should also seek God through prayer.

As He had done on previous occasions, Jesus asked that the healing of the deaf and dumb man be kept secret, but the people who had seen it were so astonished that they told it abroad. As a consequence, great multitudes followed Jesus to the summit of a hill overlooking the Sea of Galilee. There they brought the lame, the blind, and the maimed to the Great Physician, and He healed them all.

For three days Jesus stayed with them, teaching and healing. So great were the crowds that gathered to hear His teaching that their food supply ran out. Once more He fed a multitude (four thousand) with seven loaves and a few small fish (Mk. 8:1-9).

A different reception awaited Jesus on His return to Galilee. In contrast to the enthusiasm and gratitude of the people in Decapolis, He was met by a group of Pharisees and Sadducees, who demanded "a sign from heaven" (Mt. 16:1). Up to this time the Sadducees, who were not deeply religious, had shown little interest in Jesus' ministry. Their interests were largely political. On this occasion, however, they joined the Pharisees in questioning Him. The latter had already discovered that the most effective weapon that could be used to discredit Jesus was to ask for a "sign." If He were the Son of God, as He claimed to be, surely He could give them some spectacular performance that would prove His claim. They discounted His great healings by saying that He was in league with Beelzebub and they knew by this time that He would not perform any great feats to satisfy their curiosity. However, His consistent refusal gave them opportunities to poison the people's minds against Him. His reply to their demand for a sign was:

"When it is evening, you say, 'It will be fair weather; for the sky is red.' And in the morning, 'It will be stormy today, for the sky is red and threatening.' You know how to interpret the appearance of the sky, but you cannot interpret the signs of the times" (Mt. 16:2-3).

The Pharisees and Sadducees could indeed read certain signs, but they could not see that the Messiah for whom they longed was in their midst. We must believe before we can discern the works of Jesus Christ.

"Do you ask for a sign of power? Do you want miraculous healing without fulfilling the law of right thinking and right doing? Then you are not receiving the Christ spirit rightly. You are seeking the temporal instead of the eternal, and if you let this superficial phase of mind rule, you will reject the Christ spirit and cast it out of your midst" (MD 347).

Jesus left Galilee and went to Caesarea Philippi. No hostility had been aroused toward Him there, and it was His intention to quietly instruct the Twelve. As He crossed the Sea of Galilee Jesus cautioned His companions to "beware of the leaven of the Pharisees and Sadducees" (Mt. 16:6). His companions understood that He wanted them to shun the false teaching of these religious leaders so that it would not come into their consciousness where it might expand unawares.

At the outskirts of the little village of

Bethsaida, a blind man was brought to Jesus. This is the one recorded case of a partial healing followed by a complete healing. Jesus laid His hands on the blind man's eyes and asked, "Do you see anything?" (Mk. 8:23) The man said, "I see men; but they look like trees, walking" (Mk. 8:24). This indicates that although he could distinguish figures, his vision was distorted. Jesus again touched him, and clear vision was restored. This should encourage us to be grateful for any improvement in conditions about which we are praying. If we will continue to "pray through," the full healing will come.

"Now when Jesus came into the district of Caesarea Philippi, he asked his disciples, 'Who do men say that the Son of man is?' And they said, 'Some say John the Baptist, others say Elijah, and others Jeremiah or one of the prophets.' He said to them, 'But who do you say that I am?' Simon Peter replied, 'You are the Christ, the Son of the living God.' And Jesus answered him, 'Blessed are you, Simon Bar-Jona! For flesh and blood has not revealed this to you, but my Father who is in heaven. And I tell you, you are Peter, and on this rock I will build my church, and the powers of death shall not prevail against it' "

(Mt. 16:13-18).

By this question Jesus was testing the spiritual understanding of His Apostles. They represent the twelve spiritual faculties or powers of man, and it is the faith faculty (Peter) who declares, "you are the Christ." Jesus said that this revelation comes by faith, not by human sense ("flesh and blood"), but by the spirit of God that dwells in man ("my Father who is in heaven"). Charles Fillmore states:

"This revealment of Truth direct from Spirit is the rock upon which the one and only church of Jesus Christ is built. All other authorities are spurious" (TT 103).

He says further:

"The true church of Christ is a state of consciousness in man, but few have gone so far in the realization as to know that in the very body of each man and woman is a temple in which the Christ holds religious services at all times: 'Ye are a temple of God.' The appellation was not symbolical, but a statement of architectural truth. Under the direction of the Christ, a new body is constructed by the thinking faculty in man; the materials entering into this superior structure are the spiritualized organic substances, and the new creation is the temple or body of Spirit'' (TT 105).

To Peter (faith) Jesus gave ''the keys of the kingdom of heaven, and whatever you bind on earth shall be bound in heaven, and whatever you loose on earth shall be loosed in heaven'' (Mt. 16:19). As regards this teaching, Mr. Fillmore says:

''That Peter today stands at the gate of heaven is no mere figure of speech; he always stands there when you have acknowledged the Christ, and he has the 'keys of the kingdom of heaven.' The keys are the thoughts that he forms, the words that he speaks. He then stands porter at the door of thought and freely exercises that power which the Christ declares: 'Whatever you bind on earth shall be bound in heaven . . . . '

''You can see readily why this faith-thinker, Peter, is the foundation; why the faith faculty should be guarded, directed, and trained. His words are operative on many planes of consciousness, and he will bind you to conditions of servitude if you do not guard his acts closely.

"Persons who let their thinking faculty attach itself to the things of earth are limiting or binding their free ideas, or 'heaven,' and they thereby become slaves to hard, material conditions, gradually shutting out any desire for higher things.

"Those who look right through the apparent hardships of earthly environments and persistently declare them not material, but spiritual, are loosing them in the ideal or 'heaven,' and such conditions must, through the creative power vested in the thinker, eventually rearrange themselves according to His word" (MD 517).

Jesus then began to prepare His Apostles for His trial in Jerusalem. "The Son of man must suffer many things, and be rejected by the elders and chief priests and scribes, and be killed, and on the third day be raised" (Lk. 9:22). They did not understand Him. Peter took exception to what He said. "God forbid, Lord! This shall never happen to you" (Mt. 16:22). But Jesus rebuked the impetuous Peter, "Get behind me, Satan! You are a hindrance to me; for you are not on the side of God, but of men" (Mt. 16:23). Jesus realized that the time was not far

distant when He would be assailed outwardly;
yet He knew that He was making the overcoming
within Himself and that His death would be
followed by His resurrection. This was incomprehensible to the Apostles. They believed Him
to be the Messiah, an all-powerful ruler, and
they could not believe that His enemies were
strong enough to overthrow Him. The Apostles
reasoned that Jesus' statements about His future
must be parabolic utterances that referred to the
end of His present lowly position with the coming of a far better and more glorious position.
On several occasions when Jesus talked of the
Cross, the Apostles still did not understand.
They discussed His words among themselves but,
not realizing the spiritual significance of them,
they became ambitious and, sensing a change,
they sought positions for themselves in the new
regime they were convinced would be established.

It is difficult for the human mind to perceive
that spiritual mastery is the one goal worth striving for, and that it demands the complete surrender of self. Man must be willing to give up
natural inclinations before he can take on
spiritual characteristics. Jesus knew this. It was
the way He had chosen, and nothing could deter

Him. Yet He seemed unable to convey His intention even to those who were closest to Him. He warned them that He would be attacked, but they were not to be ashamed of Him, for He would come into the glory of the Father. Furthermore, "I tell you truly, there are some standing here who will not taste death before they see the kingdom of God" (Lk. 9:27). And indeed, the Apostles did see the kingdom when the Holy Spirit came on them at Pentecost.

The Twelve were soon to have a preview of the Master's glory. Leaving Caesarea Philippi, they journeyed north toward Mount Hermon. There Jesus went to the mountain to pray, taking with Him Peter, James, and John.

"And as he was praying, the appearance of his countenance was altered, and his raiment became dazzling white. And behold, two men talked with him, Moses and Elijah, who appeared in glory and spoke of his departure, which he was to accomplish at Jerusalem. Now Peter and those who were with him were heavy with sleep, and when they wakened they saw his glory and the two men who stood with him. And as the men were parting from him, Peter said to Jesus, 'Master, it is well that we are here; let us

make three booths, one for you and one for
Moses and one for Elijah'—not knowing what he
said. As he said this, a cloud came and overshadowed them; and they were afraid as they
entered the cloud. And a voice came out of the
cloud, saying, 'This is my Son, my Chosen;
listen to him!' And when the voice had spoken,
Jesus was found alone'' (Lk. 9:29-36).

The value of the Transfiguration is in its symbolic meaning. Jesus Himself referred to it as a
vision and told the Apostles not to speak of it
until after His resurrection (Mt. 17:9). Since He
was sustained by faith (Peter), judgment
(James), and love (John), He attained such a
high state of consciousness that light shone from
Him and about Him. With Jesus, representing
the Christ, were the law (Moses) and the prophetic utterances (Elijah). Obedience to the
truths given by the law and the prophets is the
process by which we rise to the Christ consciousness. Faith (Peter) is so impressed by the specta-
cle that it wants to preserve the vision in concrete
form (build three booths). This is promptly rejected by the voice or inspiration of God calling
attention to His Son and commanding, ''Listen
to him.''

Of the Transfiguration Charles Fillmore states:

"Transfiguration is always preceded by a change of mind. Our ideas must be lifted from the material, the physical, to the spiritual. But first we need to realize that it is possible for us to be transfigured as well as to understand the law by which transfiguration is brought about. . . .

"In our study and application of the Christian life we all have times when we are spiritually uplifted. Such a time is marked by a form of spiritual enthusiasm, which is brought about by statements of Truth made by ourselves or others—prayers, words of praise, songs, meditations—any statement of Truth that exalts the spiritual realms of the mind. Jesus was lifted up by Peter, James, and John (faith, judgment, and love). Whenever we dwell upon these virtues and try to live up to them, they are exalted in consciousness, and they go with us to the mount of Transfiguration. You may not always realize this. You may think that the uplifting was just a passing exaltation, but it stamps itself upon your soul and body and marks the planting of a new idea in the upward trend of the whole man. . . .

"Having once seen Truth, having once had the illumination, you find that the next step is to demonstrate it and not to be cast down or discouraged by the opposite. When the crucifixion comes and you are suffering the pangs of dying error, you may cry out, 'My God, my God, why hast thou forsaken me?' forgetting for the time the promises in the mount of Transfiguration. This is when you need to realize that you are passing through a transforming process that will be followed by a resurrection of all that is worth saving'' (ASP 150-155).

When Jesus and His companions joined the nine Apostles who had waited at the foot of the mountain, they found them surrounded by a crowd of anxious people. A man from a nearby village had brought his afflicted son to be healed. When he learned that Jesus was away, he asked the Apostles for help. They were unable to help, and when Jesus appeared, the father asked Him to heal the child. Jesus said:

" 'Bring him [the child] to me.' And they brought the boy to him; and when the spirit saw him, immediately it convulsed the boy, and he fell on the ground and rolled about, foaming at the mouth. And Jesus asked his father, 'How long has he had this?' And he said, 'From childhood. . . . but if you can do anything, have pity on us and help us.' And Jesus said to him, 'If you can! All things are possible to him who believes.' Immediately the father of the child cried out and said, 'I believe; help my unbelief!' And when Jesus saw that a crowd came running together, he rebuked the unclean spirit, saying to it, 'You dumb and deaf spirit, I command you, come out of him, and never enter him again.' And after crying out and convulsing him terribly, it came out, and the boy was like a corpse; so that most of them said, 'He is dead.' But Jesus took him by the hand and lifted him up, and he arose'' (Mk. 9:19-27).

Jesus made it plain that the father's faith was necessary for the healing of this affliction of long duration. "All things are possible to him who believes." Through faith we open ourselves to the healing currents of life that await our acceptance but which cannot be utilized unless we believe. The father did believe in spiritual healing, for he brought his son to Jesus; yet he knew that his faith was wavering. His heartfelt cry, "I believe; help my unbelief," was the reaching out for a greater faith and the unshakable assurance that Spirit is all-powerful and ever ready to supply our needs.

The Apostles who had been unable to heal the child were puzzled and dismayed at their lack of power. Had they not gone forth "two by two" and done great works in His name? When they were alone with Jesus they asked Him for an explanation of their failure in this instance. His reply was, "This kind cannot be driven out by anything but prayer" (Mk. 9:29). Prayer is a positive taking on of spiritual ideas from the Christ mind; fasting in a spiritual sense is refraining from destructive thought. Jesus' explanation answers the question that comes to those of us who think that we have sufficient faith and who want to do the healing works of the Lord, but often fail. This statement tells us that we have not yet given enough time to prayer or to denial and affirmation. The faithful practice of denial repudiates the error thoughts in consciousness. The consistent practice of affirmations steadies the mind so that the power of God can move through us to heal even deep-rooted mental and physical ailments.

Jesus' return to Capernaum was designedly secret. He did not intend to teach the multitudes again, for He desired to give His time to the training of the Twelve. However, when they reached the city, messengers from the Temple in Jerusalem, whose duty it was to collect the annual Temple tax, saw Peter and asked him if his Master would pay the tax. It was the custom for every Jew over twenty years of age living in Palestine or in foreign countries to pay a tax of half a shekel for the ransom of his soul unto the Lord, and also for the maintenance of the Temple in the Holy City. The tax produced vast sums of money that were conveyed to Jerusalem by messengers who were appointed by the Sanhedrin. Peter was accustomed to paying the tax and perhaps almost subconsciously answered for Jesus also. Then he went to Jesus to get the money.

Jesus may have been amused that He was asked to pay a tax for the ransom of His soul, and He teased Peter some by saying, "What do you think, Simon? From whom do kings of the earth take toll or tribute? From their sons or from others?" (Mt. 17:25). The answer was obvious, and Peter replied, "From others." Jesus pointed out, "Then the sons are free."

Peter had no rejoinder. Surely, the Father's son, whom Peter believed Jesus to be, should not have to pay a tax that was paid by sinners! This is one of the occasions on which we get a glimpse of

the human side of Jesus and His cordial relationship with His Apostles. He knew that He had
Peter in a corner, as it were, but He would not
desert His friend in his hour of need. Jesus then
said:

"Go to the sea and cast a hook, and take the
first fish that comes up, and when you open its
mouth you will find a shekel; take that and give
it to them for me and for yourself" (Mt. 17:27).

This miracle emphasizes the fact that divine
substance is at hand to meet all needs. When we
are in tune with the Christ we always know just
what to do in order to bring needed substance
into visibility. Gold in the fish's mouth tells us
that plenty exists in the most unexpected places.
We should never limit supply to channels that
we know of, but should keep our consciousness
receptive to the idea of abundance in order that
good can manifest in any of God's ways.

In the days that followed, Jesus often spoke of
His impending death and resurrection. It is
significant that He never spoke of death without
resurrection. We are inclined to speak of death as
a finality. When the consciousness is truly one
with God, death is a prelude to resurrection. The

Apostles failed to comprehend Jesus' meaning and discussed among themselves their relative positions in His coming kingdom. They finally asked Him the direct question, "Who is the greatest in the kingdom of heaven?" (Mt. 18:1)

"And calling to him a child, he put him in the midst of them, and said, 'Truly, I say to you, unless you turn and become like children, you will never enter the kingdom of heaven. Whoever humbles himself like this child, he is the greatest in the kingdom of heaven. Whoever receives one such child in my name receives me' " (Mt. 18:2-5).

What a lesson in humility this is! The kingdom is not for those who strive to outdo others; it is for those who have the simplicity, eagerness, and faith of a child. We are children as far as spiritual understanding is concerned. Unless we are humble, reverent toward God, and willing to listen and obey, we cannot receive the gifts He has for us.

As Jesus was talking with them, the apostle John, who revealed his ignorance of Jesus' compassion for all men, said:

" 'Teacher, we saw a man casting out demons in your name, and we forbade him, because he was not following us.' But Jesus said, 'Do not forbid him; for no one who does a mighty work in my name will be able soon after to speak evil of me. For he that is not against us is for us. For truly, I say to you, whoever gives you a cup of water to drink because you bear the name of Christ, will by no means lose his reward'' (Mk. 9:38-41).

We should recognize and commend good done by others, even those who do not share our beliefs. All good is of God. What difference does it make who does it or what he believes? People who do the works of the Father are really one in spirit.

"Then Peter came up and said to him, 'Lord, how often shall my brother sin against me, and I forgive him? As many as seven times?' Jesus said to him, 'I do not say to you seven times, but seventy times seven' '' (Mt. 18:21-22).

And He told them the parable of the unmerciful servant (Mt. 18:23-35). It teaches the lesson that when we cannot do as we should, that is, cannot fulfill the obligations that are rightly expected of us, we quickly ask forgiveness and receive it. But how do we treat people who fail to fulfill their obligations to us? Are we harsh and unforgiving? If so, our own deficiencies cannot be overlooked. When it seems that people harm us, it is only because we are looking at situations with our material eyes. Our good is always secure, for it is in God, who is ever with us. When, therefore, we appear to be wronged by others (our brother sins against us), we are to forgive "seventy times seven," or an unlimited number of times.

"We must forgive as we would be forgiven. To forgive does not simply mean to arrive at a place of indifference to those who do personal injury to us; it means far more than this. To forgive is to give for—to give some actual, definite good in return for evil given. . . .

"The very pain that you suffer, the very failure to demonstrate over some matter that touches your own life deeply, may rest upon just this spirit of unforgiveness that you harbor toward the world in general. Put it away with resolution" (LT 14).

CHAPTER IX

Later Judean Ministry
(Third Year)

It was autumn, and many Galileans were preparing to go to the Feast of Tabernacles in Jerusalem. On the eve of their departure to attend this feast, "His brethren" urged Jesus to go to Judea. Though these brethren did not believe in Him, He was an outstanding figure, and they could not understand why He kept Himself in obscurity. "Show yourself to the world," they said. Jesus refused. "My time has not yet come." However, after they had left, Jesus did go to Jerusalem, "not publicly, but in private" (Jn. 7:4-10). He knew the trip would be a dangerous one for Him and, probably, He did not want to involve others in what might occur.

The trip led through Samaria, and Jesus sent the apostles James and John to make arrangements for lodging in a village. The Samaritans refused to receive Him because He was on His way to Jerusalem, and the haughty bearing of the Jerusalem Jews had caused the Samaritans to hate them. The Samaritans' lack of hospitality so angered the two apostles that they said, "Lord, do you want us to bid fire come down from heaven and consume them?'' But Jesus rebuked them, and they went on to another village (Lk. 9:54-56).

James represents the quality of judgment; John represents the quality of love. Both of them acted in a very unspiritual fashion in this instance. Until our twelve spiritual faculties, represented by the Apostles, have been redeemed, they oftentimes go awry, even though we are walking in the Way as well as we can. It is almost encouraging to see in this instance a limited expression of our inherent powers of judgment and love (James and John), because they often have a limited expression in us! When our judgment wants to condemn and our love temporarily leaves and is replaced by a desire to destroy, we need not be discouraged. Instead, we should listen and learn from the great Teacher.

The thousands of Jews who flocked to Jerusalem for the Feast of Tabernacles were eager to see Him. ''Where is he?'' they asked (Jn. 7:11). In the midst of the celebrations Jesus appeared in the Temple and began teaching the people. They marveled at what He said, and asked, ''How is it that this man has learning, when he has never studied?'' (Jn. 7:15) Jesus had not attended the rabbinical schools in Jerusalem, yet He spoke with wisdom and authority that far surpassed that of the great scholars:

"My teaching is not mine, but his who sent me; if any man's will is to do his will, he shall know whether the teaching is from God or whether I am speaking on my own authority. He who speaks on his own authority seeks his own glory; but he who seeks the glory of him who sent him is true, and in him there is no falsehood" (Jn. 7:16-18).

The all-knowing Christ mind in us will teach us when we are willing to listen, but we must lay aside our own beliefs if we would learn from our Father.

Jesus went on to say that in one sense the Jews knew the law which Moses had given them, yet in another sense they were pitiably ignorant of it. Then He asked them bluntly, "Why do you seek to kill me?" (Jn. 7:19) He knew that the Jewish leaders had sent men to take Him, but the people generally were unaware of this and asked who was threatening His life. Without answering, Jesus reminded them that in accordance with the Mosaic law a man could be circumcised on the

Sabbath; but that they were angry when He healed a man on the Sabbath. He admonished them, "Do not judge by appearances, but judge with right judgment" (Jn. 7:24).

This verse on judgment has an exceedingly important teaching that we should remember. Any appearance of limitation is deceptive, for God is omnipresent. It is wise to look for reality beyond every negative appearance, and spiritual perception makes it possible for us to do this. We may see divine order that is beyond the display of disorder, love that is beyond the show of hate, and wholeness that is beyond the manifestation of disease. To behold the good that exists in the very midst of any appearance of evil is indeed to "judge with right judgment."

On the last and great day of the feast, Jesus again attempted to convince His countrymen that His was a divine mission.

"If any one thirst, let him come to me and drink. He who believes in me, as the scripture has said, 'Out of his heart shall flow rivers of living water.' Now this he said about the Spirit, which those who believed in him were to receive" (Jn. 7:37-39).

After His declaration some said that Jesus was

a prophet, and others accepted Him as the Christ. But some wondered how the Christ could be a Galilean, when the Scriptures said that He would be of the seed of David and would come from the city of Bethlehem.

"So there was a division among the people over him. Some of them wanted to arrest him, but no one laid hands on him" (Jn. 7:43-44).

Up to this time only the Pharisees had opposed Jesus, but now the Sadducees, the second most important party among the Jews, joined with them in active hostility toward Him. Though they were smaller in number than the Pharisaic party, the Sadducees were the aristocracy. They openly courted the favor of the Romans and had been rewarded with great political power. The Pharisees' enmity for Jesus came from the fear that He would destroy their sacred law, but the Sadducees, who were far more material in their interests, paid scant attention to Him until it was evident that He was gaining much influence over the masses. At last, considering Him a religious fanatic, the Sadducees decided that it would be better to have Him out of the way, for He might stir up trouble in Palestine and jeopardize their prestige and authority. Therefore, the Sadducees acted with the Pharisees and sent officers from the Sanhedrin, the supreme court of the Jews, to bring Jesus before this court for trial.

The Sanhedrin, located in Jerusalem, was composed of seventy-one members selected from prominent Sadducees and Pharisees. The high priest was appointed by the Roman government and was invariably a Sadducee. The court had jurisdiction over religious and civil matters affecting Jews, but it lacked authority to pass the death sentence.

When the officers failed to take Jesus captive, they were summoned before the Sanhedrin in order that they might explain. They declared, in excusing themselves, "No man ever spoke like this man!" (Jn. 7:46) The members of the court chided them for being "led astray," and pointed out that they, the Jewish leaders, considered Him a false prophet. Only one voice in the Sanhedrin was raised in Jesus' defense: that of Nicodemus. He reminded them that the Jewish law did not condemn a man without giving him a chance to defend himself. Sneeringly they asked, "Are you from Galilee too?" (Jn. 7:52), implying that Nicodemus was a follower of the Nazarene.

The next day Jesus returned to the Temple, where He was called on to use the wisdom and compassion of Christ in dealing with a woman taken in adultery. She was brought to Him by the scribes and Pharisees, who wanted to trick Jesus into taking a stand that would discredit Him with the people. The law of Moses prescribed death by stoning for an adulteress, but this punishment had been abandoned long before, since the Jews had become indifferent in upholding the moral code. Then, too, Judea was a Roman province and only the Roman procurator could pronounce the death verdict. However, if Jesus failed to uphold Mosaic law, the people would not consider Him a prophet. If He did uphold it, He would show Himself pitiless, and, in addition, would break the Roman law.

"Jesus bent down and wrote with his finger on the ground. And as they continued to ask him, he stood up and said to them, 'Let him who is without sin among you be the first to throw a stone at her.' . . . But when they heard it, they went away, one by one, beginning with the eldest, and Jesus was left alone with the woman standing before him. Jesus looked up and said to her, 'Woman, where are they? Has no one condemned you?' She said, 'No one, Lord.' And Jesus said, 'Neither do I condemn you; go, and do not sin again' '' (Jn. 8:6-11).

Jesus never condoned vice of any kind.

His wisdom in handling this case teaches us that there is always a way to work out complex situations in line with Principle. "Do not sin again," He said, yet He was compassionate of sinners. He knew that the persons who condemned the woman were guilty of many evils and He gave them opportunity to see themselves in their true light. At the same time, He gave the woman opportunity to live a better life in the future. Sometimes it seems that we must choose between a cruel act and upholding wrongdoing. Only the Christ can tell us how to act in accordance with Principle, and when we do everyone is benefited.

During the Feast of Tabernacles the people, the priests, and the Pharisees joined in festal dances to the music of flutes and other instruments. The Levites stood on the fifteen steps leading to the court and chanted the majestic Psalms known as the Songs of Ascents (Ps. 120-134). Lighted by gigantic candelabra some fifty cubits in height and splendidly gilded, the scene was a very impressive one. Undoubtedly, the memory of its splendor lingered long in the minds of all who witnessed it.

In this setting, Jesus later gave the teaching in which He referred to Himself as the light of the world:

"I am the light of the world; he who follows me will not walk in darkness, but will have the light of life" (Jn. 8:12).

The Pharisees immediately took exception to His words. The spiritually illumined mind, which Jesus represents, and the limited human mind, represented by the Jewish leaders, are in sharp conflict. They speak a different language, and neither can understand the other. The things of the Spirit must be spiritually discerned, and so long as a person is in the Pharisaic state of consciousness he is not able to see beyond the literal interpretation of religion. Thus, the Christ word is incomprehensible. Jesus said to them:

"You are from below, I am from above; you are of this world, I am not of this world. . . . for you will die in your sins unless you believe that I am he. . . . When you have lifted up the Son of man, then you will know that I am he, and that I do nothing on my own authority but speak thus as the Father taught me'' (Jn. 8:23-28).

It is only when our consciousness is raised to the higher realm (the Son of man is lifted up) that we recognize and understand the word of one who speaks from the Christ level.

As Jesus spoke, ''many believed in him'' (Jn. 8:30). To them He said:

''If you continue in my word, you are truly my disciples, and you will know the truth, and the truth will make you free'' (Jn. 8:31-32).

We are the children of God and have within us the divine life of our Father. Unless we hold to this true view and obey the promptings of Spirit within, we cannot gain real freedom.

But the Jews insisted that they were already free. They claimed that they were ''Abraham's seed'' and therefore were not in bondage to any man.

''Truly, truly, I say to you, every one who commits sin is a slave to sin. The slave does not

continue in the house for ever; the son continues
for ever. So if the Son makes you free, you will
be free indeed'' (Jn. 8:34-36).

Charles Fillmore states:

''The 'house' is man's body. No one who al-
lows intemperate desires to rule his life and to
gain expression through his thought and conduct
can hope to remain long in the body or to experience in it any measure of true satisfaction. Only
the 'Son,' the self-forgetting, loving, helpful
concentration of all the powers on the gaining of
a higher understanding of the forces that control
mankind, can bring full and complete freedom.
Once this power of concentration is gained and
practiced, perfect freedom is indeed assured. But
concentration does not spring, perfect and full-
fledged, from beneath the fleeting wing of the
random resolve; it requires the faithful giving of
oneself to the practice of the presence of God.
'Abideth' entails a continuing in the Christ state
of mind and heart'' (MJ 88).

Surely ''Abraham's children'' would be righteous, they insisted, thus showing their dependence on human ancestry. Jesus reminded them

that if they were Abraham's children in the true sense of the word, they would do his works. Instead, the Jews sought to kill Jesus, who taught Truth as He received it from God. "If God were your Father, you would love me, for I proceeded and came forth from God" (Jn. 8:42). "Truly, truly, I say to you, if any one keeps my word, he will never see death" (Jn. 8:51).

The words of Jesus were more powerful than those of any other man, but here the word as used means the creative Word of God, the Logos. Jesus "infused the divine-life idea into His words until they made direct union with the creative Word of the Father" (MJ 93).

Charles Fillmore goes on to say:

"When man in faith makes this intimate connection between his mind and the Father's, he enters into what may be termed the 'river of life,' and he has ability to take others with him into the waters that cleanse, purify, and vitalize so perfectly that death is swallowed up in life and man lives right on without the tragedy of death. Such a man was, and is, Jesus the Christ, and the promise is that all who incorporate in mind and body the living creative Word, as He did, will with Him escape death. This promise of the

overcoming power of the Word has been interpreted to mean death of the soul after physical
death, but there is no foundation for this assumption. Jesus overcame death of the body. His
followers are expected to do the same'' (MJ 93).

To the Jews, Jesus' statement was quite
unreasonable. They knew that Abraham and the
prophets were dead. ''Who do you claim be?''
they demanded.

''Jesus answered, 'If I glorify myself, my glory
is nothing; it is my Father who glorifies me, of
whom you say that he is your God. But you have
not known him . . . . but I do know him and I
keep his word. Your father Abraham rejoiced
that he was to see my day' '' (Jn. 8:54-56).

The Jews reminded Jesus that He was not yet
fifty years of age, and they refused to believe that
He had seen Abraham. Jesus replied, ''Truly,
truly, I say to you, before Abraham was, I am''
(Jn. 8:58).

Jesus was speaking from the plane of the
Christ, the everlasting self of humanity, without
beginning and without end. The Christ existed
before humans came into being and will exist

throughout the eons of time. He is spiritual man, created in God's image and likeness. Jesus knew Himself to be one with Christ, and He declared His eternal livingness.

The Jews were so angered by Jesus' statement that they picked up stones to throw at Him, but He hid Himself and went out of the Temple.

"As he passed by, he saw a man blind from his birth. And his disciples asked him, 'Rabbi, who sinned, this man or his parents, that he was born blind?' Jesus answered, 'It was not that this man sinned, or his parents, but that the works of God might be made manifest in him. We must work the works of him who sent me, while it is day; night comes, when no one can work. As long as I am in the world, I am the light of the world.' As he said this, he spat on the ground and made clay of the spittle and anointed the man's eyes with the clay, saying to him, 'Go, wash in the pool of Siloam' (which means Sent). So he went and washed and came back seeing" (Jn. 9:1-7).

When the people saw the man who had been healed of blindness, they were amazed, and asked him who had restored his sight. When he replied that he did not know, he was taken to the Pharisees to whom he told his story. It was the Sabbath, and some of the Pharisees said, "This man [the healer] is not from God, for he does not keep the sabbath" (Jn. 9:16). But several asked how a sinner could do such marvelous works, and some suggested that perhaps the man had not really been blind from birth. So they sought out his parents and questioned them. His parents testified that their son had been born blind, but they knew nothing of how his healing had come about. "Ask him; he is of age." This the Pharisees did, and tried to make him retract his story. They insisted that only God could heal, and that surely a sinner could not have opened his eyes. The man's firm response was: "Whether he is a sinner, I do not know; one thing I know, that though I was blind, now I see" (Jn. 9:25). The Jews then became so angry that they cast the man out of the Temple.

The Apostles' question, "Who sinned, this man or his parents, that he was born blind?" reveals the Jewish belief that distress of body or circumstances was the direct result of disobedience to God's law—sin. Was the man's blindness caused by his own sin? This blindness did not result from a sin that was committed during his life, for he had been blind at birth. The question shows the general acceptance of reincarnation among the Jews, which holds that the sins of a former life are outpictured as difficulties in a person's present existence. However, as the man had not overcome the condition growing out of the failures of a previous life, he was guilty of what Charles Fillmore calls a "sin of omission":

"Before he was healed, the blind man was a sinner of omission. He was a blind beggar, a person who had no perception of his own capacity, or no confidence in his power to rise superior to conditions in the material realm. When man fails to apprehend his mission and to do the work of bringing forth the good that is allotted to him, he remains in darkness. His blindness is that sin of omission which is present in every man who does not realize his Place in the Godhead. If a man fails to do that which he is told from within is the right thing to do, he is sinning, and his soul will remain in darkness to just the degree that he sins" (MJ 97).

The second part of the question asks if the sins of the man's parents were responsible for this affliction. To this day many people believe in in-

herited weaknesses. Although we now know that
there are genetic *tendencies*, we continue to
uphold the power of Spirit to overcome even
these. Jesus refuted them also. He saw in the
condition an opportunity to bring forth the
wholeness that God ordained for humankind
("the works of God should be made manifest in
him"). When we are in bondage to some form
of limitation, be it physical or mental, it does little good to argue as to who was at fault. Is it not
far better to have faith that the healing can and
will come through?

"The works of God that we are to make manifest are the perfect ideas of a perfect-man idea in
Divine Mind. 'Ye therefore shall be perfect, as
your heavenly Father is perfect.' We are to bring
forth in ourselves the perfection of Being. If
through neglect, laziness, or belief in inability
we fail to do this, we fall under the judgment of
the constantly operating law of life, which is inwardly urging us and in all the visible and invisible forms of nature is commanding, 'Go forward.'

"The world is full of people who are in this
beggarly blind state. They sit by the wayside and
wait for the workers to give them pennies and

crusts, when they themselves might be the pro-
ducers of their own good. The remedy for their
situation is for them to deny material darkness,
ignorance, and inability in themselves. By putting the clay upon the blind man's eyes Jesus
illustrated how man makes opaque his understanding by affirming the power of material conditions to hamper and impede his spiritual and
material growth. The washing away of this clay
by the man himself shows that by our own voli-
tion and our own efforts we must deny away
these seeming mountains of environing conditions'' (MJ 97-98).

Hearing that the Pharisees had driven the man
from the Temple, Jesus located him, and the
man affirmed his faith in Jesus as the Son of
God. When we take our stand with Christ, the
Pharisees in our mental realm oppose us and try
to convince us that we are doing something
wrong (put us out of the Temple). If, however,
we hold to our spiritual conviction, we shall continue to see clearly and shall worship God in
spirit and in Truth. The mortal thoughts are
blind, and Jesus took this occasion to give the
Pharisees a lesson on true and false teachers:

"Truly, truly, I say to you, he who does not enter the sheepfold by the door but climbs in by another way, that man is a thief and a robber; but he who enters by the door is the shepherd of the sheep. To him the gatekeeper opens; the sheep hear his voice, and he calls his own sheep by name and leads them out. When he has brought out all his own, he goes before them, and the sheep follow him, for they know his voice. A stranger they will not follow, but they will flee from him, for they do not know the voice of strangers" (Jn. 10:1-5).

The I AM (Christ) is the good Shepherd who tenderly cares for His sheep (thoughts). The thoughts that enter our minds "some other way" than by the door (spiritual inspiration) are thieves and robbers (error thoughts). Christ's sheep (spiritual ideas) know the voice of the Shepherd (I AM) and follow Him. When strangers (error thoughts) come and would destroy them, the sheep do not hear them. "I am the good shepherd. The good shepherd lays down his life for the sheep" (Jn. 10:11).

"This means that the high spiritual I AM lets itself become identified with the limitations of self-consciousness that it may lift all up to the spiritual plane. 'I lay down my life, that I may take it again.'

"When we open the door of the mind by consciously affirming the presence and power of the divine I AM in our midst, there is a marriage or union of the higher forces in being with the lower, and we find that we are quickened in every part; the life of the I AM has been poured out for us. Thus Christ becomes the Savior of the whole world by pouring this higher spiritual energy (His blood) into human consciousness, which each must take for himself and identify himself with. The individual I AM is the only door through which it can get into our thoughts in a legitimate way. If it comes through mediumship or hypnotism or mental suggestion, without our willing cooperation, it is 'a thief and a robber' " (MJ 101-102).

When Jesus had concluded His teaching on the good Shepherd:

"There was again a division among the Jews because of these words. Many of them said, 'He has a demon, and he is mad; why listen to him?' Others said, 'These are not the sayings of one

who has a demon. Can a demon open the eyes of
the blind?' " (Jn. 10:19-21)

The difference of opinion among the Jews
about Jesus signifies the uncertainty of the mind
in its human intellectual state. It argues back
and forth, swinging from belief in Christ to rejection of Him.

Jesus realized that nothing further could be
accomplished in Jerusalem, and He returned to
Galilee for a brief stay. A short time later, He appointed seventy disciples to go on a missionary
tour. The word *disciple* was often used to designate people who believed in Jesus and accepted
His teaching. They were His general followers.
The word *apostle* was applied to the twelve men
whom Jesus called and who accompanied Him
during the three years of His ministry. Jesus
"sent them [the seventy disciples] on ahead of
him, two by two, into every town and place
where he himself was about to come" (Lk. 10:1).

Jesus' instructions to the seventy disciples were
similar to those He gave to the Apostles (see
Chapter VII). When they returned, probably
several weeks later, they were exceedingly joyous,
and said:

" 'Lord, even the demons are subject to us in your name!' And he said to them, 'I saw Satan fall like lightning from heaven. Behold, I have given you authority to tread upon serpents and scorpions, and over all the power of the enemy; and nothing shall hurt you. Nevertheless do not rejoice in this, that the spirits are subject to you; but rejoice that your names are written in heaven' " (Lk. 10:17-20).

When we go forth "in His name" and feel spiritual power operating through us, we are happy and grateful. Jesus' remark that He "saw Satan fall like lightning from heaven" means that error thoughts (Satan), which have invaded the harmony of mind (heaven), are dislodged by the spiritual word. By holding fast to Truth we have power over conditions that would ordinarily injure us (serpents, scorpions, and the enemy). Jesus warns, however, that we are not to rejoice in the outer demonstration itself but, rather, to rejoice that we have attained a greater degree of spiritual awareness and authority (our names are written in heaven).

The last six months of Jesus' ministry were to mark an increasing hostility on the part of Jewish leaders and a more stern mood on His part. He traveled rapidly from place to place, going several times into Judea. On one of these brief visits, a scribe (called a lawyer in the Bible text), thinking to confuse Jesus, asked:

" 'Teacher, what shall I do to inherit eternal life?' He said to him, 'What is written in the law? How do you read?' And he answered, 'You shall love the Lord your God with all your heart, and with all your soul, and with all your strength, and with all your mind; and your neighbor as yourself.' And he said to him, 'You have answered right; do this, and you will live.' But he, desiring to justify himself, said to Jesus, 'And who is my neighbor?' " (Lk. 10:25-29)

In answer to this question, Jesus gave one of the most beautiful of the parables, the parable of the Good Samaritan (Lk. 10:30-37). Our neighbor is anyone who is nearby and needs assistance, whether friend or stranger. We cannot expect to correct all the ills of the world but we can help the people with whom we come in contact. This is our spiritual service. Sometimes this need is satisfied by a kind or inspiring word; sometimes physical aid is necessary. Often our most effective service is to pray for others. It is not by chance that certain people come into the orbit of our lives. They are drawn to us by the law of attraction, and we should not, like the priest and the Levite, pass by "on the other side." According to the Jews, a Samaritan was inferior racially and religiously; but he was more truly spiritual than those of whom righteousness was expected. Jesus Himself was playing the part of the Good Samaritan by telling this parable to a Jewish scribe who, bound by the letter of the law, could easily overlook its spirit.

Finally Jesus reached Bethany, a small village a few miles to the south of Jerusalem. In this village lived His three friends, Martha, Mary, and their brother Lazarus. The three comprised a family in easy circumstances, and of sufficient dignity and position to excite considerable attention in their own village and even in Jerusalem, as was proved later when Lazarus was raised from the dead. Martha welcomed Jesus and began to prepare a feast for her renowned guest; Mary "sat at the Lord's feet and listened to his teaching" (Lk. 10:39).

"But Martha was distracted with much serving; and she went to him and said, 'Lord, do you not care that my sister has left me to serve alone?

Tell her then to help me.' But the Lord answered her, 'Martha, Martha, you are anxious and troubled about many things; one thing is needful. Mary has chosen the good portion, which shall not be taken away from her' '' (Lk. 10:40-42).

Women represent the emotional or feeling nature, and the two sisters symbolize love operating on different levels. Martha's love was expressed by ministering to the physical needs of Jesus whereas Mary's love bade her listen to His words. It is good to serve in an outer way, but it is better still to take time to sit at the Lord's feet and give attention to what He says (study and pray). Jesus commended Mary, for she had chosen the higher office of love, which is worship. "One thing is needful," He said. That one thing is what we should have above all else, even to this day—a devotion to Christ and a willingness to devote some time to the contemplation of that which is divine.

"He was praying in a certain place, and when he ceased, one of his disciples said to him, 'Lord, teach us to pray, as John taught his disciples' '' (Lk. 11:1).

The verses that follow in The Gospel According to Luke record a shorter form of The Lord's Prayer than the one given in the Sermon on the Mount (Mt. 6:9-13). Jesus expanded His teaching on prayer by giving the parable of the importunate friend (Lk. 11:5-8). This parable emphasizes the necessity of persistence in prayer. Our Father is not reluctant to answer our requests, but we often have to ask Him a number of times in order to develop the faith that will enable us to receive. Jesus gave the assurance of answered prayer in the words:

"Ask, and it will be given you; seek, and you will find; knock, and it will be opened to you. For every one who asks receives, and he who seeks finds, and to him who knocks it will be opened" (Lk. 11:9-10).

Then Jesus showed the similarity between the love of our heavenly Father and that of an earthly father. If the earthly father loves his children and wants to give them good gifts, "how much more will the heavenly Father give the Holy Spirit to those who ask him!" (Lk. 11:13)

While Jesus was still in Judea, He again denounced the scribes and Pharisees, "for you tithe

mint and rue and every herb, and neglect justice
and the love of God; these you ought to have
done, without neglecting the others'' (Lk.
11:42). As Jesus was speaking, a crowd gathered
about Him. However, He addressed Himself to
the Twelve, warning them, "Beware of the
leaven of the Pharisees, which is hypocrisy" (Lk.
12:1). Hidden sins will come to light. Jesus said,
"Nothing is covered up that will not be revealed, or hidden that will not be known" (Lk.
12:2). Whatever abides in our consciousness
must manifest itself eventually. We cannot prevent destructive thoughts from outpicturing in
our bodies and circumstances.

A person in the crowd asked Jesus to compel
his brother to divide an inheritance with him.
Jesus refused and said, "Take heed, and beware
of all covetousness; for a man's life does not con-
sist in the abundance of his possessions" (Lk.
12:15). To illustrate His point, Jesus gave the
parable of the rich fool (Lk. 12:16-21). The person who lays up treasures for himself and ne-
glects his spiritual obligations is shortsighted and
foolish. When men leave the body they cannot
take material possessions with them, but they are
compelled to take the consciousness that they
have acquired. If we have given time and

thought to gaining spiritual treasures—under-standing, love, and peace—we are "rich toward God," and He will see that we lack no good thing. "Fear not, little flock, for it is your Fa-ther's good pleasure to give you the kingdom" (Lk. 12:32).

Jesus followed this teaching with another para-ble, the parable of the waiting servants (Lk. 12:35-40). It brings out the lesson that we should keep our consciousness so constructive ("let your loins be girded and your lamps burn-ing") that we will be ready for a spiritual realiza-tion (our Lord) at any time, "for the Son of man is coming at an unexpected hour."

In further explanation of the preceding para-ble, Jesus told the parable of the wise steward (Lk. 12:41-48). We are stewards, appointed by our Lord to do His work in the world. When we are faithful in the performance of our tasks, the Father gives us authority and dominion ("he will set him over all his possessions"). If, on the other hand, we disregard His commandments and foolishly think that there will not be a day of reckoning, "the master of that servant will come on a day when he does not expect him . . . and will punish him, and put him with the unfaith-ful." The Lord represents the law of cause and effect, always operative and rendering to each person his just deserts. When we understand God's requirements and fail to fulfill them, our punishment from the law is severe, for "every one to whom much is given, of him will much be required."

About this time word was brought to Jesus that a resistance movement against the Roman government had been detected by Pontius Pilate, and a number of Galileans had been slain. Jesus gave the group a warning against wrongdoing of any kind. He intimated that the Galileans who had perished because they revolted against Rome were no more sinful than others, even those dwelling in Jerusalem who prated of their piety. "I tell you, No; but unless you repent you will all likewise perish" (Lk. 13:3).

The parable of the barren fig tree (Lk. 13:6-9) illustrates His point. Unless we practice the principles of right thinking and acting, we are like a fig tree that bears no fruit. Our failure to produce spiritually separates us from our Lord, and we are worthless ("Why should it use up the ground?"). Jesus, whose mission was to save humankind, is likened to the vinedresser who pleaded with the owner of the vineyard to spare the tree for a time, that he might give it special care in the hope that it would bring forth figs. It seemed that even at this time in His ministry Jesus still hoped that the Jews would accept Him and rectify their lives. This parable reminds us that even though we may have failed to put our spiritual resources to good use, our Father is still patient and gives us another chance.

As Jesus traveled about the country He often taught in a synagogue on the Sabbath.

"And there was a woman who had had a spirit of infirmity for eighteen years; she was bent over and could not fully straighten herself. And when Jesus saw her, he called her and said to her, 'Woman, you are freed from your infirmity.' And he laid his hands upon her, and immediately she was made straight, and she praised God" (Lk. 13:11-13).

This healing is unusual in that the woman did not ask for it. It brings out the thought that when we turn to God (symbolized by the woman's attending a religious service), we can be benefited in ways we do not foresee. The lifted consciousness is what makes us receptive to divine blessings; by seeking God we invariably find some portion of His good.

CHAPTER X

Perean Ministry

(Third Year)

There was a great rejoicing in Jerusalem, for it was again time for the Feast of the Dedication. This feast, held each winter, and lasting eight days, commemorated the cleansing of the Temple by Judas Maccabaeus in 165 B.C., after it had been profaned by the King of Syria.

The eastern porch of the Temple was called Solomon's Porch, because it was built of material that had been preserved from the original Temple. Here Jesus was walking on the porch when He was surrounded by a group of Jews who asked:

" 'How long will you keep us in suspense? If you are the Christ, tell us plainly.' Jesus answered them, 'I told you, and you do not believe. The works that I do in my Father's name, they bear witness to me' " (Jn. 10:24-25).

"By their fruits ye shall know them," was the substance of Jesus' words. He had done great works that could be done only by one who knew

''I and the Father are one'' (Jn. 10:30). However, to the Jewish leaders His words were blas-
phemous, and again they took up stones to slay
Him.

''Jesus answered them, 'I have shown you
many good works from the Father; for which of
these do you stone me?' The Jews answered him,
'It is not for a good work that we stone you but
for blasphemy; because you, being a man, make
yourself God' '' (Jn. 10:32-33).

Jesus reminded them that their Scriptures
said, ''You are gods'' (Ps. 82:6). Why, then, did
they refuse to believe Him when He claimed to
be divine?

''If I am not doing the works of my Father,
then do not believe me; but if I do them, even
though you do not believe me, believe the
works, that you may know and understand that
the Father is in me and I am in the Father'' (Jn.
10:37-38).

Spiritual works are the natural expression of
one established in the realization of oneness with
Christ. But those persons who consider them-

selves religious and yet cannot heal or perform so-called miracles are at a loss to understand the person who can. In their ignorance they bitterly oppose him and seek to belittle what he does.

The Jews tried again to take Jesus, but they could not. Perhaps something of the majesty of His being deterred them. After the Feast of Dedication "he escaped from their hands" (Jn. 10:39), retiring to the section of Palestine known as Perea, east of the Jordan and across the river from Judea.

It was now only three or four months until the Passover, at which time Jesus would be crucified. During these months Jesus traveled from place to place, going into Judea on several occasions. His days were filled with teaching and good works. Contests with His enemies were sharper, and the conditions He imposed for discipleship were more stringent. Much of His instruction was presented through parables, thirteen of which were given in these last few months. The raising of Lazarus was the outstanding event in this period, and Jesus' lifted consciousness, which was evident at this time, was a fitting prelude to His resurrection.

As Jesus went through a Perean village He was asked, "Lord, will those who are saved be few?'' His answer was, "Strive to enter by the narrow door; for many . . . will seek to enter and will not be able" (Lk. 13:23-24). The narrow door signifies that those who wish to "enter in" must strictly adhere to spiritual principle; otherwise, they will be shut out, and "there you will weep and gnash your teeth, when you see Abraham and Isaac and Jacob and all the prophets in the kingdom of God and you yourselves thrust out" (Lk. 13:28). There is nothing harsh or unjust about this adherence. The law of God that governs our lives is exact, and unless we comply with this law we cannot expect to receive its rich benefits.

Wherever Jesus went, the Pharisees kept a watchful eye on Him. One Sabbath a ruler of the Pharisees invited Him to dinner. The critical attitude of the guests caused Jesus to tell the parable of the guests at feasts (Lk. 14:7-11), a lesson in true humility. Jesus explained that the most important guest at a banquet should have the seat of honor next to the host (chief seat), but instead of waiting to be invited, the Jews would often lose all sense of decorum and struggle for the coveted place. Jesus taught that a person should select the lowest seat (humble himself), and then wait to be moved higher (be exalted). He pointed out that a person can easily lose worldly prestige when he is striving for the chief place and is then forced to take the lowest place. The feeling of insecurity and selfishness in each of us is revealed when we push ourselves forward. Our true worth ensures us an honorable place without any effort on our part.

" 'For every one who exalts himself will be humbled, and he who humbles himself will be exalted.' He said also to the man who had invited him, 'When you give a dinner or a banquet, do not invite your friends or your brothers or your kinsmen or rich neighbors, lest they also invite you in return, and you be repaid. But when you give a feast, invite the poor, the maimed, the lame, the blind, and you will be blessed, because they cannot repay you. You will be repaid at the resurrection of the just' " (Lk. 14:11-14).

We are not to give with the hope of getting something in return, but we are to help others who are less fortunate than ourselves. The law of love rewards us.

One of the guests at the ruler's dinner remarked, "Blessed is he who shall eat bread in the kingdom of God'' (Lk. 14:15), and in answer Jesus told the parable of the great supper (Lk. 14:16-24). From it we learn that we are all invited to God's feast (an abundance of divine ideas). Do we consent to partake of it or do we make excuses? The person who is absorbed in materiality slights the things of Spirit (''I have bought a field, and I must go out and see it''). The person who is enslaved by his animal tendencies also turns aside (''I have bought five yoke of oxen, and I go to examine them''). The one who loves personality revels in the joy of it and refuses to give his attention to God (''I have married a wife, and therefore I cannot come''). The persons who are in trouble (''the poor and maimed and blind and lame'') are glad to accept the Lord's bounty. The derelicts (those who are found in the ''highways and hedges'') are compelled to come to the feast. Persons who have reached the lowest level in life can turn to God. In so doing they appropriate divine ideas (eat of the feast) and are nourished, whereas those who make excuses cannot ''taste of my supper.''

As the multitudes followed Him, Jesus cautioned them to count the cost before they decided to become His disciples.

"If any one comes to me and does not hate his own father and mother and wife and children and brothers and sisters, yes, and even his own life, he cannot be my disciple. Whoever does not bear his own cross and come after me, cannot be my disciple. . . . So therefore, whoever of you does not renounce all that he has cannot be my disciple" (Lk. 14:26-27, 33).

These are powerful words, and they have often been misinterpreted. They mean that when we desire to tread the spiritual path we must put God before any human relationships and even before life itself. By so doing we do not neglect our responsibilities to our families. Rather, we fulfill them more fully because we give prime consideration to our Lord and draw wisdom and love from Him. To bear our cross is to take upon ourselves the task of eliminating the qualities in us that do not measure up to a spiritual ideal. We must carefully consider the price to be paid for spiritual enlightenment and power.

Jesus further illustrated the requirements for discipleship in the parable of the tower and the king (Lk. 14:28-33). A wise man does not attempt to build a tower without first making sure that he can complete it. Neither would a wise king undertake to conquer an army without first considering whether he had sufficient strength to win the battle. Likewise, if we expect to build spiritual strength (a tower) or overcome adverse thoughts (an army), we must be certain of the firmness of our resolve and of our willingness to cooperate with Spirit in order that Spirit may express through us. In other words, we must put love of God before anything else.

"Now the tax collectors and sinners were all drawing near to hear him. And the Pharisees and the scribes murmured, saying, 'This man receives sinners and eats with them' " (Lk. 15:1-2).

In rapid succession Jesus gave three parables in defense of His compassion for and interest in sinners. These are the parables of the lost sheep, the lost coin, and the prodigal son.

In the parable of the lost sheep (Lk. 15:3-7), Jesus taught the love of the Christ (owner of the sheep) for His children, good and bad (all the sheep). The lost sheep represents the person who has strayed from the path of righteousness, yet the owner (the Christ) leaves the sheep that are safe in the fold (the ninety and nine) and seeks the one that is lost. When He finds him there is great rejoicing. "I tell you, there will be more joy in heaven over one sinner who repents than over ninety-nine righteous persons who need no repentance" (Lk. 15:7).

The parable of the lost coin (Lk. 15:8-10) expands the idea that every individual is important to Christ. The lost coin symbolizes the erring person who must be diligently sought until recovered. The owner of the coin is the one who searches for it, even as the Christ always seeks to reclaim the lost. There is rejoicing "over one sinner who repents."

Perhaps the best known and loved of Jesus' parables is that of the prodigal son (Lk. 15:11-32). The younger son symbolizes the person who has not yet been awakened to his spiritual nature and who takes his inheritance (divine substance) from his father (God) and departs into a "far country" (material consciousness). There he squanders his resources of mind and body in sense gratification ("squandered his property in loose living"), and the inevitable result is depletion ("want"). Because man is innately spiritual, he gradually awakens to his true nature (the prodigal "came to himself") and realizes that happiness and fulfillment can come only by a reunion with God ("I will arise and go to my father"). The prodigal is aware of his sins, seeks forgiveness, and shows his willingness to return to his father's house and take a lowly position. "Father, I have sinned against heaven and before you; I am no longer worthy to be called your son." But God is love, and love is extended to the repentant one regardless of his iniquities. "While he was yet at a distance, his father saw him and had compassion, and ran and embraced him and kissed him." As the prodigal makes contact with the divine source, abundance of good flows forth. His father gives him the best robe, a ring, shoes, and an opulent feast. "For this my son was dead, and is alive again; he was lost, and is found."

The elder brother was unforgiving and harsh in judging his brother, and showed no pleasure in his return. He was jealous of his father's blessing extended to one whom he considered unworthy. He was envious of his brother's good fortune and his reinstatement in the home. He was sullen and angry, and would not attend the feast. Like the Pharisees to whom Jesus told the parable, the elder brother was self-righteous. "Lo, these many years I have served you, and I never disobeyed your command." No one is less merciful than he who is unaware of any fault in himself. Persons who know they have fallen short of goodness and ask forgiveness come into the kingdom more quickly than those whose eyes are closed to their own shortcomings. Yet the elder brother is also a child of God and is reminded of his right to share in His good. "Son, you are always with me, and all that is mine is yours."

Jesus told three parables on stewardship after He had finished the parables that showed His great interest in sinners. The first, the parable of the unjust steward, was given to some disciples; the second, the parable of the rich man and Lazarus, to the Pharisees; and the third, the parable of the unprofitable servant, to the Apostles.

The lesson contained in the parable of the unjust steward (Lk. 16:1-13) is frequently misunderstood, for it seems that Jesus commended the dishonesty of the steward. In this parable Jesus was teaching His followers that they were to have the responsibility of discharging a spiritual service to the people without His personal guidance. He was keenly aware that His disciples were still men of the world and not sufficiently acquainted with or trained in the principles of spiritual thinking and action. Jesus, therefore, depicted a trickster, a man well versed in methods used in the marts of trade where the dictum is that the end justifies the means. The unjust steward adhered faithfully to the only standard he knew. Jesus was not approving the dishonest act but was commending the consistency with which the steward operated. His god was mammon, whom he served devotedly and well. "The sons of this world are more shrewd in dealing with their own generation than the sons of light" (Lk. 16:8).

Those who accept Jesus are called "sons of light"; yet, are they as loyal to this higher standard as the "sons of this world" are to theirs? "If then you have not been faithful in the unrighteous mammon, who will entrust to you the true riches?" (Lk. 16:11) If the disciples had not complied with the best they understood before embarking on the spiritual way, how could they be trusted with a higher responsibility? They should not vacillate between the Christ idea and the world's ideal, for "no servant can serve two masters; for either he will hate the one and love the other, or he will be devoted to the one and despise the other. You cannot serve God and mammon" (Lk. 16:13).

"The Pharisees, who were lovers of money, heard all this, and they scoffed at him. But he said to them, 'You are those who justify yourselves before men, but God knows your hearts; for what is exalted among men is an abomination in the sight of God' " (Lk. 16:14-15).

Then Jesus told the Pharisees the parable of the rich man and Lazarus (Lk. 16:19-31). Charles Fillmore gives an interpretation of this parable as follows:

"Jesus describes the states of consciousness of one who passes through the change called death. The rich man and Lazarus represent the outer and inner consciousness of the average worldly minded man and woman. The outer consciousness appropriates the attributes of soul and body and expresses them through sense avenues. 'He was clothed in purple and fine linen, faring sumptuously every day.' This condition typifies material riches.

"Material selfishness starves the soul and devitalizes the psychical body. This body is described thus: 'A certain beggar named Lazarus was laid at his gate, full of sores, and desiring to be fed with the crumbs that fell from the rich

man's table.' The soul life is put out of the consciousness and fed with the dogs.

"When death overtakes such a one [the rich
man], the inner as well as the outer life changes
environment. The material avenues are lost to
the outer, and the soul finds self in a hell of
desires without the flesh sensations through
which to express itself. 'And in Hades he lifted
up his eyes, being in torments.'

"Lazarus, the beggar, was 'carried away by the
angels into Abraham's bosom.' The inner spiritual ego, drawn by its innate spiritual ideas,
finds a haven of rest in the bosom of the Father,
represented by Abraham.

"When man loses the material avenues of expression and has not developed the spiritual, he
is in torment. Appetite longs for satisfaction,
and in its anguish for a cooling draught calls to
its spiritual counterpart (Lazarus). But the body
consciousness, the place of union for all the attributes of man, has been removed, producing in
the life consciousness a great gulf or chasm that
cannot be crossed, except by incarnation in
another body.

"Then the sense man is contrite, and would
have his five brothers warned of the danger of
sense life. These five brothers are the five senses.

Abraham says, 'They have Moses and the prophets; let them hear them'; that is, they understand the law (Moses) and they know what will
follow its transgression (prophets). The rich man
rejoins: 'Nay, father Abraham: but if one go to
them from the dead, they will repent.' And He
said unto him, 'If they hear not Moses and the
prophets, neither will they be persuaded, if one
rise from the dead.' The personal consciousness,
which has been formed through material attachments, cannot be reached except through its own
plane of consciousness. The phenomenal manifestations of spiritualism do not cause people to
repent of their sins'' (TT 155-157).

When the Apostles were alone with Jesus they
made a request of Him: ''Increase our faith!''
(Lk. 17:5) To this He replied:

''If you had faith as a grain of mustard seed,
you could say to this sycamine tree, 'Be rooted
up, and be planted in the sea,' and it would
obey you'' (Lk. 17:6).

Jesus followed these words with the parable of
the unprofitable servants (Lk. 17:7-10). Its lesson
is that no one is to be praised for doing what his

work requires. "So you also, when you have done all that is commanded you, say, 'We are unworthy servants; we have only done what was our duty.' " Each of us has personal responsibilities to discharge, but if that is all we do, we are indeed "unworthy servants." It is only when we go beyond the personal and fulfill our obligation to God in love, obedience, and service that we are rewarded with the faith that accomplishes mighty things.

While Jesus was still in Perea He received word from His beloved friends, Martha and Mary, that their brother Lazarus was sick. "But when Jesus heard it he said, 'This illness is not unto death; it is for the glory of God, so that the Son of God may be glorified by means of it'' (Jn. 11:4), and He remained in Perea two more days. Then, knowing that Lazarus had died, Jesus and His Apostles went to Bethany (in Judea). The sorrowing sisters greeted Him. They believed that if Jesus had been with them Lazarus would not have died. Jesus said:

"I am the resurrection and the life; he who believes in me, though he die, yet shall he live, and whoever lives and believes in me shall never die" (Jn. 11:25-26).

Then Jesus asked to be led to Lazarus' tomb, and He had the stone removed.

"And Jesus lifted up his eyes and said, 'Father, I thank thee that thou hast heard me. I knew that thou hearest me always, but I have said this on account of the people standing by, that they may believe that thou didst send me.' When he had said this, he cried with a loud voice, 'Lazarus, come out.' The dead man came out, his hands and feet bound with bandages, and his face wrapped with a cloth. Jesus said to them, 'Unbind him, and let him go' " (Jn. 11:41-44).

Of this outstanding miracle Charles Fillmore states:

"Jesus represents man in the regeneration; that is, man in the process of restoring his body to its natural condition, where it will live right on perpetually without old age, disease, or death. A necessary step in this process of body restoration is the quickening of the sleeping Lazarus, who represents the vitalizing energies in the subconsciousness that feed the body and give it the life force that renews its youth. . . .

"Bringing this sleeping life to outer consciousness is no easy task. Jesus groaned in spirit and was troubled at the prospect. The higher must enter into sympathy and love with the lower to bring about the awakening—'Jesus wept.' But there must be more than sympathy and love—'Take ye away the stone.' The 'stone' that holds the sleeping life in the tomb of matter in subconsciousness is the belief in the permanency of present material laws. This 'stone' must be rolled away through faith. The man who wants the inner life to spring forth must believe in the reality of omnipresent spiritual life and must exercise his faith by invoking in prayer the presence of the invisible but omnipresent God. . . .

"In Spirit all things are fulfilled now. The moment a concept enters the mind, the thing conceived is consummated through the law that governs the action of ideas. . . . The spiritual-minded take advantage of this law and affirm the completeness of this ideal, regardless of outer appearances. This stimulates the energy in the thought process and gives it power beyond estimate. This is the step that Jesus took when He lifted up His eyes and said: 'Father, I thank thee that thou heard me. And I knew that thou hearest me always.' The sleeping youth (Lazarus) does not at once respond, but the prayer of thanksgiving that is now in action gives the assurance that calls it at the next step to the surface—'Lazarus come forth.'

"Jesus 'cried with a loud voice.' This emphasizes the necessity of working strenuously to project the inner life to the surface. . . .

"Freedom from all trammels is necessary before the imprisoned life can find its natural channel in the constitution. 'Loose him, and let him go' means unfettered life expressing itself in joyous freedom of Spirit" (MJ 109-112).

Many Jews who were friends of the family had come to Bethany to be with Martha and Mary after Lazarus had died, and these witnessed his resurrection. Some of them believed that Jesus was indeed the Messiah, but others were antagonistic and reported the happenings to the Jewish leaders in Jerusalem. The Sanhedrin met promptly to consider how best to handle a situation that the members felt was rapidly getting out of hand. They could not deny the miracle but, on the other hand, they could not believe in the one who performed it. They dreaded Jesus' growing influence with the people, for they thought He would use His power to try to make Himself a king and thus cause a Roman army to be sent to Judea. Such action would, of course, endanger the Sadducees' political power. Finally Caiaphas, the high priest, said, "You know nothing at all; you do not understand that it is expedient for you that one man should die for the people, and that the whole nation should not perish" (Jn. 11:49-50). Definite plans to apprehend Jesus were set into operation, and from that time He lived with a price upon His head. He was not ignorant of what was going on, and withdrew to the village of Ephraim in the northern part of Judea. Here Jesus and His Apostles remained until near the time for the Feast of the Passover, when He went through Samaria and into southern Galilee.

On the outskirts of one of the villages, Jesus and His Apostles met a group of ten lepers. The Mosaic law required that lepers keep a certain distance from other persons and cry "unclean" when anyone approached them. When they saw Jesus the lepers pleaded, "Jesus, Master, have mercy on us" (Lk. 17:13).

"When he saw them he said to them, 'Go and show yourselves to the priests.' And as they went they were cleansed. Then one of them, when he saw that he was healed, turned back, praising God with a loud voice; and he fell on his face at Jesus' feet, giving him thanks. Now he was a Samaritan. Then said Jesus, 'Were not ten cleansed? Where are the nine? Was no one found to return and give praise to God except this foreigner?' And he said to him, 'Rise and go your way; your faith has made you well' '' (Lk. 17:14-19).

In Jesus' time leprosy was a common disease, especially among the poorer classes. Since it was left to the priests to decide whether the victim was actually afflicted with leprosy or had some minor skin disease, only the priests could pronounce a leper clean and thus re-establish him in the community life. Jesus' command to the lepers that they show themselves to the priests was tantamount to saying that they were healed and would receive a clean bill of health from the proper authorities.

The spiritual significance of this miracle is that when we turn to the Christ spirit within us and faithfully pray, we may be healed immediately. When we receive this blessing are we then so elated that we forget to thank God? If so, the healing is quite likely to be temporary, for we have failed to connect it with spiritual power. The leper who returned to glorify God was the only one whose permanent healing was certain. He knew the source from which it came and returned to express his gratitude.

Soon after His encounter with the ten lepers, Jesus gave two parables on prayer: the parable of the importunate widow (Lk. 18:1-8) and the parable of the Pharisee and the publican (Lk. 18:9-14). The first stresses again the necessity of persistence in prayer. No analogy exists between the unjust judge and God, for God does not fail to answer prayer. He is never weary of our pleas. The lesson lies in the fact that we "ought always to pray and not lose heart" (Lk. 18:1), and in turning again and again to our Father we become responsive to the blessings He always has for us.

In the parable of the Pharisee and the publican Jesus draws a contrast between the prayer of the self-righteous individual and that of the humble penitent. The Pharisee was proud of his piety, which made him feel superior to other men. The publican offered his prayer in meekness of spirit. He was aware of his shortcomings and sought mercy. "I tell you, this man went down to his house justified rather than the other;

for every one who exalts himself will be humbled, but he who humbles himself will be exalted'' (Lk. 18:14).

Jesus and His Apostles soon left Galilee for the
last time. Crossing the Jordan, they entered
Perea, and it became known that Jesus was not to
remain long. Many parents brought their children to Him "that he might lay his hands on
them and pray" (Mt. 19:13). When the Apostles
rebuked these parents for disturbing the Master,
Jesus was indignant and said:

"Let the children come to me, do not hinder
them; for to such belongs the kingdom of God.
Truly, I say to you, whoever does not receive the
kingdom of God like a child shall not enter it"
(Mk. 10:14-15).

After He had lovingly gathered the little children to Him, Jesus laid His hands on them and
blessed them.

One day a young man of great wealth and
high position came to Jesus. He was apparently
convinced that Jesus could explain the meaning
and mystery of life. He prostrated himself before
the Master, crying, "Good Teacher, what must I
do to inherit eternal life?" (Mk. 10:17) Jesus

reminded him that only God is good, and asked if he were obeying the commandments. The young man assured Him that he was.

"And Jesus looking upon him loved him, and said to him, 'You lack one thing; go, sell what you have, and give to the poor, and you will have treasure in heaven; and come, follow me'' (Mk. 10:21).

With His marvelous power of discernment, Jesus saw that the young man's heart was attached to his riches, even though he had some desire for the things of Spirit. The prime requirement of spiritual living is to put God first, and that was the real meaning of Jesus' words to the young man. Jesus did not recommend poverty, but He always made it plain that spiritual attainment demands that love for God come first. When the young man "went away sorrowful; for he had great possessions" (Mk. 10:22), Jesus said to His Apostles:

"Children, how hard it is to enter the kingdom of God! It is easier for a camel to go through the eye of a needle than for a rich man to enter the kingdom of God" (Mk. 10:24-25).

Those who have great wealth are apt to give more importance to it in their lives than they give to spiritual things. So long as they do they cannot attain godliness.

Peter reminded Jesus that the Twelve had "left everything" and followed Him, and he questioned, "What then shall we have?" Jesus replied that those who had put personal interests aside "for my name's sake, will receive a hundredfold, and inherit eternal life. But many that are first will be last, and the last first" (Mt. 19:29-30).

Since Jesus wanted to emphasize that God is no respecter of persons, and gives to all alike, He told the parable of the laborers in the vineyard (Mt. 20:1-16), in which God is likened to the householder who is hiring laborers to work in His vineyard (God's workers in the world). To each of the persons who labored, even those who were hired the sixth, the ninth, and the eleventh hour, the householder gave the same pay—a shilling. The shilling represents all that we need in the way of supply. It makes no difference when we accept Truth and begin to work with God. We may have known the joy of serving Him for many years. Yet even the beginner in God's work may draw on the infinite resources of

Spirit. People who have served God for a long time are sometimes apt to be envious of the good a beginner receives (the laborer who comes in at the eleventh hour), but the Lord says, ''I choose to give to this last as I give to you'' (Mt. 20:14). The true Christian will rejoice in this knowledge.

The time for the Feast of the Passover was approaching, and Jesus and His Apostles joined a group of Galilean pilgrims who were on their way to Jerusalem. As they walked along the road, Jesus said to the Twelve:

''Behold, we are going up to Jerusalem; and the Son of man will be delivered to the chief priests and scribes, and they will condemn him to death, and deliver him to the Gentiles to be mocked and scourged and crucified, and he will be raised on the third day'' (Mt. 20:18-19).

This was the most concise prophecy that Jesus had uttered, and the Apostles still did not understand. Only a short time later, Salome, the mother of James and John, approached Him with the request that her sons sit '' 'one at your right hand and one at your left, in your kingdom.' But Jesus answered, 'You do not know what you are asking. Are you able to drink the

cup that I am to drink?' '' (Mt. 20:21-22),
meaning the trial He was to undergo. James and
John answered that they were able, showing a
complete lack of understanding of the events
that were to come.

"He said to them, 'You will drink my cup,
but to sit at my right hand and at my left is not
mine to grant, but it is for those for whom it has
been prepared by my Father'' (Mt. 20:23).

The Master knew that the Apostles soon would
suffer some of the things He had endured and
was yet to endure. But neither He nor any other
man could give them, nor can He give us today,
the fruits of the kingdom. Glory and honor are
for persons who attain the consciousness of
oneness with God and receive from Him what
He in love has prepared for them.

When the other Apostles heard of the plea for
special favors made on behalf of James and John,
they were angry. Jesus, calling them to Him,
gave the Twelve a lesson on spiritual greatness:

"You know that the rulers of Gentiles lord it
over them, and their great men exercise authority over them. It shall not be so among you; but

whoever would be great among you must be your servant, and whoever would be first among you must be your slave; even as the Son of man came not to be served but to serve, and to give his life as a ransom for many'' (Mt. 20:25-28).

In a spiritual sense a great person is one who is completely willing to serve, seeking not to be ministered to but to minister to others. As we develop a consciousness of Spirit we take on the qualities of Spirit, the chief of which is to pour itself out in service to humankind. ''To give his life as a ransom for many'' does not refer to Jesus' crucifixion, but to the great spiritual service He rendered during the years of His ministry. He gave Himself unreservedly in order that others could know the Truth that would make them free.

As the pilgrims came near Jericho, Jesus was accosted by a blind beggar whose name was Bartimaeus. (Mark and Luke mention only one blind man in their gospels, whereas Matthew's gospel mentions two. The miracles may be the same.) The Apostles tried to silence the beggar, but he continued to cry out. Jesus then directed that Bartimaeus be brought to Him. When he was asked what he wanted, the blind man replied, "Let me receive my sight," and Jesus said, "Go your way; your faith has made you well" (Mk. 10:51-52).

Metaphysically Bartimaeus represents:

"A phase of the darkened mentality in man. This blinded, polluted and poverty-stricken state of mind is the outcome of the race habit of attributing honor and precedence to old established beliefs and customs . . . to the exclusion of present spiritual inspiration. But this darkened, contaminated-with-error phase of the mentality is groping for light, which is realized through Jesus Christ, the Word of God expressed" (MD 98).

It was necessary for travelers to rest at Jericho before entering the dangerous, rocky, robberhaunted gorge that led from it to Jerusalem. Jericho, near the Dead Sea, is six hundred feet below the Mediterranean Sea level, and Jerusalem is nearly three thousand feet above it, necessitating an almost continuous ascent for some six hours. A colony of publicans was established in Jericho, and they collected revenues from people who carried on a large traffic in buying and selling a kind of balsam that grew luxuriously in the hot, humid climate. The publicans also regulated the exports and imports between Judea, ruled by the Roman governor, and Perea, ruled by Herod Antipas. One of these chief publicans was the extremely wealthy Zacchaeus, a Jew, hated even by his own people for extorting exorbitant taxes from them. When Zacchaeus heard that Jesus was passing through Jericho, he wanted to see Him. This presented a difficulty, however, for Zacchaeus was short of stature and he could not see over the heads of the crowd that surrounded the Nazarene. Determined to see Jesus, Zacchaeus climbed a sycamore tree, and as Jesus passed by He looked up and said to him, "Zacchaeus, make haste and come down; for I must stay at your house today" (Lk. 19:5). This Zacchaeus did, and his contact with Jesus resulted in his complete reformation.

" 'Behold, Lord, the half of my goods I give to the poor; and if I have defrauded any one of anything, I restore it fourfold.' And Jesus said to him, 'Today salvation has come to this house, since he also is a son of Abraham. For the Son of man came to seek and to save the lost' " (Lk. 19:8-10).

The name Zacchaeus means "purified, just, righteous." These pertain to qualities that are the divine attributes of all people, but a person's character may be perverted by an excessive love for material things. Such a person becomes greedy and unjust. The mission of the Christ is to save. When a person answers His call ("Zacchaeus, make haste, and come down"), entertains Him, and listens to His word, a transformation takes place in his or her life ("the half of my goods I give to the poor").

After they left Jericho, the Apostles still thought that Jesus was going to Jerusalem to set up the kingdom of God on earth. It was at this time that Jesus told them the parable of the pounds (Lk. 19:12-27). Jesus represents the nobleman of the parable, who is going away to receive a kingdom. He will return, even though His countrymen hate Him and oppose His rule. Nevertheless, He had given each of His ten servants a gift (a spiritual quality that is symbolized by a pound). Each servant was to be rewarded in proportion to what use he made of his gift. The servant who increased his gift was to receive greater authority and also greater responsibility, while he who permitted his gift to lie dormant was to be deprived of it.

This parable teaches that each one is given opportunity to take the gift of Truth that Christ gives. Those who accept Truth and abide by His words (increase their gift) will develop their innate spirituality, and their reward will be a greater understanding and spiritual power. Those who reject Truth (refuse to use their gift) will lose their capacity for spiritual expression.

" 'I tell you, that to every one who has will more be given; but from him who has not, even what he has will be taken away.' . . . And when he had said this, he went on ahead, going up to Jerusalem" (Lk. 19:26, 28).

CHAPTER XI

Holy Week

The Gospels vividly depict events that occurred in the last days of Jesus' earthly life.

On Friday evening, six days before the Feast of the Passover, Jesus and the Apostles arrived in Bethany and visited at the home of Lazarus, Martha, and Mary. Here many persons came, "not only on account of Jesus but also to see Lazarus, whom he had raised from the dead" (Jn. 12:9).

On the following Sunday (which we now call Palm Sunday) Jesus and the Twelve left Bethany on foot to journey to Bethphage. As they neared the village Jesus sent two of the Apostles on ahead, telling them to bring back a colt they would find there. The Apostles did as they were instructed and, throwing their garments upon the colt, they put Jesus thereon. A multitude had now gathered, and the procession started for Jerusalem.

"Most of the crowd spread their garments on the road, and others cut branches from the trees and spread them on the road. And the crowds that went before him and that followed him shouted, 'Hosanna to the Son of David! Blessed is he who comes in the name of the Lord! Hosanna in the highest!' and when he entered Jerusalem, all the city was stirred, saying, 'Who is this?' And the crowds said, 'This is the prophet Jesus from Nazareth of Galilee' '' (Mt. 21:8-11).

Jesus' ride into Jerusalem created quite a sensation, but it was a fulfillment of the prophecy of Zechariah: ''Rejoice greatly, O daughter of Zion! Shout aloud, O daughter of Jerusalem! Lo, your king comes to you; triumphant and victorious is he, humble and riding on an ass, on a colt the foal of an ass'' (Zech. 9:9). Jesus knew the prophecy, and this was His way of telling the people that He was their king and that He was just and lowly, even though He had brought salvation to the world through the Word of God.

Metaphysically Jesus' action symbolizes the mastery of the I AM over the animal nature:

''The characteristics of the ass are meekness, stubbornness, persistency, and endurance. To ride these is to make them obedient to one's will. The outer thoughts, or people, recognize that some unusual movement of mind is going on, and they fall into line. Their cry, 'Hosanna,' means *save now*. A change of base from personal willfulness to meekness and obedience stirs the whole consciousness, or city, and there is questioning about the cause. Simply saying in the silence, 'Not my will, but thine, be done,' often stirs up a commotion, and then there is questioning as to the cause. The answer is, 'This is the prophet (one who states the spiritual law), Jesus (the I AM), from Nazareth (place of development) of Galilee (life activity).' Rendered in modern metaphysical terms this would read, 'This is the supreme I AM stating the law of Spirit in development of life action' '' (MD 348).

The Gospel According to Luke gives additional information as regards the triumphal journey to Jerusalem. Some Pharisees were among the many people who followed Jesus and, probably frightened by the enthusiastic shouts of the multitude, said to Him, ''Teacher, rebuke your disciples'' (Lk. 19:39). Jesus replied, ''I tell you, if these were silent, the very stones would cry out'' (Lk. 19:40), meaning that it was indeed appropriate for the people to give honor to their Messiah and that even the inanimate stones would protest if the people were too blind to acclaim Him.

The procession could not proceed beyond the foot of Mount Moriah, upon which the Temple stood. Here the crowd dispersed, and Jesus and the Apostles entered the Temple. "And the blind and the lame came to him in the temple, and he healed them" (Mt. 21:14). This, together with the people's cry, "Hosanna to the son of David," was the same as acknowledging Jesus as the Messiah.

The chief priests and scribes were so angry that they reprimanded Him. "Do you hear what these are saying?" Jesus answered them adroitly, "Yes; have you never read, 'Out of the mouth of babes and sucklings thou hast brought perfect praise'?" (Mt. 21:16) Thus we find that spiritual Truth is often hid from the learned and revealed to the lowly who have more faith.

Sunday afternoon Jesus and the Twelve returned to Bethany. Here with their loved friends they spent the nights during Holy Week, walking to Jerusalem each day, a distance of about four miles.

On Monday morning, as Jesus and His companions set out for Jerusalem, He "hungered."

"And seeing a fig tree by the wayside he went to it, and found nothing on it but leaves only. And he said to it, 'May no fruit ever come from you again!' " (Mt. 21:19)

The barren fig tree symbolizes unfruitful conditions in our life. All of us need to bring forth the fruits of our spiritual nature, just as it is the function of the fig tree to produce figs. When we discover that a certain state of mind is not constructive and is the parent of unwholesome conditions, it is our right to "curse" or deny it. By the power of the word spoken in faith, we can "wither" these sterile states of mind and their attendant negative appearances and thus be free of them.

The Apostles were surprised to see the fig tree dying immediately, and Jesus said to them:

"Truly, I say to you, if you have faith and never doubt, you will not only do what has been done to the fig tree, but even if you say to this mountain, 'Be taken up and cast into the sea,' it will be done. And whatever you ask in prayer, you will receive, if you have faith" (Mt. 21:21-22).

Upon reaching the Temple, Jesus saw a scene He had witnessed three years before. There was great confusion. The outer court was crowded with merchants selling oxen, sheep, and doves. The money-changers were arguing with those who had foreign coins to exchange. Once again Jesus cleansed the Temple, saying, "Is it not written, 'My house shall be called a house of prayer for all the nations'? But you have made it a den of robbers" (Mk. 11:17). The first cleansing of the Temple was at the beginning of Jesus' ministry, the second cleansing was just prior to His great test. This brings to mind the thought that before we undertake any spiritual project we should make certain that our consciousness is free of material beliefs and interests.

As Jesus was teaching in the Temple, some Greeks, probably Jewish proselytes attracted to Jerusalem by the Passover, asked Philip to arrange for them to have a private interview with Jesus. Philip was evidently puzzled at the request and told Andrew. Together the two apostles then informed Jesus of the request. Historically, nothing is known of these Greeks or why they wished to speak with Jesus. Instead of granting their request, Jesus spoke to the crowd at the Temple:

"The hour has come for the Son of man to be glorified. Truly, truly, I say to you, unless a grain of wheat falls into the earth and dies, it remains alone; but if it dies, it bears much fruit. He who loves his life loses it, and he who hates his life in this world will keep it for eternal life. If any one serves me, he must follow me; and where I am, there shall my servant be also; if any one serves me, the Father will honor him" (Jn. 12:23-26).

Charles Fillmore states:

"Common sense often saves a man from the fanaticism of religious enthusiasm. The Greeks represent the practical side of man's nature. They ask Philip for an interview with Jesus, and Philip tells Andrew. All this means that it is through the power (Philip) and strength (Andrew) in man that the sense reason acts, and when the I AM is called down from its lofty spiritual enthronement to the contemplation of practical life, there is a restoration of equilibrium. Then it recognizes the law of giving its exalted ideality to the earthly consciousness, that it may also be lifted up. To the higher consciousness this seems like the death of an ideal, but it is only a temporary submergence, which has its resurrection in a great increase of life and power. Thus we lose our life in the service of the good, and count it of no value in order to find it again in Spirit'' (MJ 119).

In the higher consciousness we may realize that the surrender of the mortal way of thinking paves the way for the elevation of spiritual unfoldment, but such surrender is not easy for us. Even Jesus cried out, ''Now is my soul troubled. And what shall I say? 'Father, save me from this hour'?''(Jn. 12:27) Yet even as the words left His lips there came the realization, ''No, for this purpose I have come to this hour. Father, glorify thy name'' (Jn. 12:27-28). When we have become established in spiritual consciousness, we understand that all we have striven for leads to the hour when only the Christ counts. Then our prayer is that the Father's name be glorified:

''Then a voice came from heaven, 'I have glorified it, and I will glorify it again.' The crowd standing by heard it and said that it had thundered. Others said, 'An angel has spoken to him.' Jesus answered, 'This voice has come for your sake, not for mine' '' (Jn. 12:28-30).

Thus, a voice from heaven was heard for the third time during Jesus' ministry. It had been heard at Jesus' baptism, and again on the Mount of Transfiguration. "This means that Jesus' heavenly credentials were sufficient and that there was nothing to fear. The demonstration must eventually be forthcoming" (MJ 120).

"Now is the judgment of this world, now shall the ruler of this world be cast out; and I, when I am lifted up from the earth, will draw all men to myself" (Jn. 12:31-32).

When we realize that Spirit is supreme, all the lingering falsity in our consciousness is dissolved (the ruler of this world is cast out). As we lift up the Christ within, He draws to us all that is worthy of His presence.

The people who heard these words did not understand, and Jesus, knowing the futility of attempting to explain further, only cautioned, "While you have the light, believe in the light, that you may become sons of light" (Jn. 12:36). Yet many were not able to believe. A few who understood and would have accepted Him feared that the Pharisees would excommunicate them if their belief were known, and they still "loved

the praise of men more than the praise of God''
(Jn. 12:43).

Again showing His divine authority, Jesus
said:

"He who believes in me, believes not in me
but in him who sent me. And he who sees me
sees him who sent me. I have come as light into
the world, that whoever believes in me may not
remain in darkness. If any one hears my sayings
and does not keep them, I do not judge him; for
I did not come to judge the world but to save the
world. He who rejects me and does not receive
my sayings has a judge; the word that I have
spoken will be his judge on the last day'' (Jn.
12:44-48).

After speaking these words, Jesus and the
Twelve left the Temple and returned to Bethany
for the night.

When Jesus reached the Temple on Tuesday
morning, He found a formidable deputation
awaiting Him. The chief priests, the learned
scribes, and the leading rabbis were ready to
challenge His authority as an accredited teacher.
They bitterly resented Jesus' teachings, which
were contrary to the established beliefs of

Judaism as they interpreted them. They demanded to know by what authority He taught. Jesus knew they wanted to trap Him, so instead of answering their question, He asked one: "The baptism of John, whence was it? From heaven or from men?" (Mt. 21:25) This presented a problem to the Jews. If they admitted that John's baptism was "from heaven," that He was divinely inspired, they would be conceding that Jesus was the Messiah whom John had proclaimed. On the other hand, they dared not denounce John and say that his message was "of men," for the people reverenced the Baptist, and the rejection of John would stir up much antagonism. Thus the masters of Israel were reduced to the ignominious necessity of saying, "We do not know" (Mt. 21:27). To this Jesus replied, "Neither will I tell you by what authority I do these things" (Mt. 21:27). In this and in additional contests with His opponents, Jesus displayed a superhuman intelligence that enabled Him to perceive their machinations and to counteract them.

To drive home the lesson of their spiritual blindness, Jesus gave three parables: the parable of the two sons (Mt. 21:28-32), the parable of the wicked husbandmen (Mt. 21:33-43), and the parable of the wedding feast and wedding garment (Mt. 22:1-14). Each of these shows how the Jewish leaders had failed to discharge their spiritual obligations to God and man. They were indeed blind leaders of the blind. In their personal application these parables contain great lessons for us today.

The parable of the two sons is a reminder that it is what we do, not what we say, that is the measure of our worthiness. The first son represents persons who refuse to accept and live by a spiritual standard (decline to work in the Father's vineyard), but who later repent and obey Him. The second son typifies those people who make a great boast of piety, yet do not honestly try to live righteously (they promise to work in the Father's vineyard but fail to do so). "Truly, I say to you, the tax collectors and the harlots go into the kingdom of God before you" (Mt. 21:31).

The parable of the wicked husbandmen reveals that each of us is given charge of the divine resources of spirit, soul, and body. We must render an account of our stewardship to the Lord. If selfishness, greed, fear, and cruelty have been allowed to gain control over us, we try to retain our seeming good by repudiating the things of Spirit (slay the messengers of the Lord). However, the time comes when we are compelled to realize that the Christ is supreme (head of the corner) and that our rejection of Him leads to our utter defeat.

The parable of the wedding feast and the wedding garment relates that God has prepared a feast for all and invites us to it. Those in personal consciousness make light of His invitation, and they not only pursue their worldly interests but definitely reject His summons (kill the king's messengers). The price they pay is death to the good that God has for them. Those who accept His invitation must prepare themselves properly (wear a wedding garment). Our preparation for participation in God's good consists of spiritual thinking and living. The robe of righteousness is the only fit wedding garment. Without this, we shall not be permitted to eat at His table. " 'Bind him hand and foot, and cast him into the outer darkness; there men will weep and gnash their teeth.' For many are called, but few are chosen" (Mt. 22:13-14).

Though the Jewish authorities were enraged by Jesus' parables, the meaning of which was all too obvious to them, they had by no means exhausted their efforts to discredit Him. Certain

Pharisees joined with a group of Herodians in questioning Him. The Herodians were a political party whose chief purpose was to uphold the reign of the Herods, whom the Pharisees despised. However, the Pharisees' hatred for Jesus was greater than their dislike for the Herodians and, in joining them, the Pharisees hoped that Jesus would be forced to make a statement that could be construed as disloyalty to Rome.

With words of flattery the Pharisees and Herodians approached Jesus:

" 'Teacher, we know that you are true, and teach the way of God truthfully, and care for no man; for you do not regard the position of men. Tell us, then, what you think. Is it lawful to pay taxes to Caesar, or not?' But Jesus, aware of their malice, said, 'Why put me to the test, you hypocrites? Show me the money for the tax.' And they brought him a coin. And Jesus said to them, 'Whose likeness and inscription is this?' They said, 'Caesar's.' Then he said to them, 'Render therefore to Caesar the things that are Caesar's, and to God the things that are God's' " (Mt. 22:16-21).

Again Jesus was more than a match for His

enemies' attacks. His words are a guide for the perfect balance a person should have between worldly and spiritual things. We are to render unto each its rightful due. If we are faithful to God, we shall discharge our outer obligations rightly and without difficulty.

Completely routed, the Pharisees and Herodians retired. Then came a group of Sadducees with a query. Addressing Him with mock respect, they asked a trick question concerning the Resurrection, in which they themselves did not believe.

" 'Teacher, Moses said, "If a man dies, having no children, his brother must marry the widow, and raise up children for his brother." Now there were seven brothers among us; the first married, and died, and having no children left his wife to his brother. So too the second and third, down to the seventh. After them all, the woman died. In the resurrection, therefore, to which of the seven will she be wife? For they all had her.' But Jesus answered them, 'You are wrong, because you know neither the scriptures nor the power of God. For in the resurrection they neither marry nor are given in marriage, but are like angels in heaven. And as for the resurrection of the dead, have you not read what was said to you by God, "I am the God of Abraham, and the God of Isaac, and the God of Jacob"? He is not God of the dead, but of the living' " (Mt. 22:24-32).

Jesus' answer points out that the relationship of marriage as it is known on earth does not exist beyond the grave, "for in the resurrection they neither marry nor are given in marriage." Sex is of the flesh, and when the soul leaves the body, the latter disintegrates. God is not the God of the dead body, but of the living soul.

Yet, once more the insatiable spirit of dissension awoke, and this time a scribe, a student of the Torah, tried to fathom the extent of Jesus' wisdom:

" 'Teacher, what is the great commandment in the law?' And he said to him, 'You shall love the Lord your God with all your heart, and with all your soul, and with all your mind. This is the great and first commandment. And a second is like it, You shall love your neighbor as yourself. On these two commandments depend all the law and the prophets' " (Mt. 22:36-40).

Jesus artfully combined the Ten Commandments into two. The Decalogue deals with our
right attitude toward God and our fellow human
beings. The spiritual teaching of all the religious
seers of the ages is summed up in these two commandments given by the Great Teacher. In the
Sermon on the Mount Jesus had said, "You,
therefore, must be perfect, as your heavenly
Father is perfect" (Mt. 5:48). We attain perfection by obedience to these two commandments.

Jesus now had the opportunity to question the
Jewish leaders, and His query trapped them as
they had hoped theirs would trap Him. He
asked:

" 'What do you think of the Christ? Whose
son is he?' They said to him, 'The son of David.'
He said to them, 'How is it then that David, inspired by the Spirit, calls him Lord, saying, "The
Lord said to my Lord, Sit at my right hand, till I
put thy enemies under thy feet"? If David thus
calls him Lord, how is he his son?' " (Mt.
22:42-45)

Jesus was quoting from Psalms 110, which the
Pharisees regarded as distinctly Messianic; yet,
they could think of no reply. There could be but

one answer: the Son (Messiah) was divine, not human. Jesus was David's son by natural birth, since Mary was of the house of David. But as the Messiah, He was David's Lord. The Pharisees were embarrassed, since they could not explain a matter that concerned their own religion, and they withdrew.

"Then said Jesus to the crowds and to his disciples, 'The scribes and the Pharisees sit on Moses' seat; so practice and observe whatever they tell you, but not what they do; for they preach, but do not practice' " (Mt. 23:1-3).

Jesus denounced formalism in religion in scathing words, and utterly repudiated the ambitious teachers, priests, and rabbis who care more for the praise of men than for obedience to God. His was a call to recognize one God only. After He had enumerated the faults of a religion of the letter from which the Spirit had been banished, He termed it a mockery that was doomed to destruction. There was, however, more of grief than condemnation in His words, and He concluded with the heartfelt lament over the Holy City, whose sons and daughters had turned from the loving help that He would have given them so gladly and freely:

"O Jerusalem, Jerusalem, killing the prophets and stoning those who are sent to you! How often would I have gathered your children together as a hen gathers her brood under her wings, and you would not! Behold, your house is forsaken and desolate. For I tell you, you will not see me again, until you say, 'Blessed is he who comes in the name of the Lord' " (Mt. 23:37-39).

The day was now far advanced, and it was clear that any possibility of a reconciliation between Jesus and the Jewish leaders was gone. As He was leaving the Temple for the last time, He passed through the Court of the Women. In this court were thirteen chests, called "shoperoth," each shaped like a trumpet, into which the people were casting their contributions:

"He looked up and saw the rich putting their gifts into the treasury; and he saw a poor widow put in two copper coins. And he said, 'Truly I tell you, this poor widow has put in more than all of them; for they all contributed out of their abundance, but she out of her poverty put in all the living that she had' '' (Lk. 21:1-4).

God does not require from us the sacrifice of material necessities; yet, when we love Him enough to deprive ourselves of some pleasure in order to support His ministry, our gift has much more worth than its monetary value. Likewise, it means more than the gifts of those who, from the abundance they have, share only a small portion. As we give freely in appreciation for the many blessings the Lord has bestowed on us, our consciousneses expands and becomes a magnet for the attraction of additional good to ourselves. However, the expression "the widow's mite" has come to mean more than a contribution of money. It represents the giving of our all—love, obedience, service—in His name. This is what our Father asks of us. In return He gives unstintingly of Himself.

As Jesus and the Apostles left the Temple, they turned and gazed once more at all its splendor. It was a magnificent structure, one of the wonders of the ancient world. The Temple had a number of beautiful gates. One was of solid Corinthian brass, and the others were overlaid with gold and silver. The building had graceful and towering porches, beveled blocks of marble, cloisters and stately pillars, with rising terraces of courts that led to the topmost court, the Holy of Holies. And as Jesus beheld this beauty, He was sad. He knew that little sincerity existed in the hearts of the majority of the worshipers, and without this the Temple could not be a house of prayer. It was already doomed, and He said to His companions, ''You see all these, do you not? Truly, I say to you, there will not be left here one stone upon another, that will not be thrown down'' (Mt. 24:2).

Forty years later this prophecy about the Temple was fulfilled literally, for in A.D. 70, the Roman general Titus had it completely destroyed. However, at the time that Jesus spoke, Judea was at peace with Rome. This prophecy apparently frightened the Apostles, and they were silent as they left Jerusalem. After they had crossed the valley of Kidron, Jesus and the Twelve climbed the steep path that led to the Mount of Olives. When they had sat down to rest, the Apostles asked, ''Teacher, when will this be, and what will be the sign when this is about to take place?'' (Lk. 21:7)

Jesus answered these questions in the Olivet Discourse, or the Great Eschatological Discourse, recorded in Matthew 24 and 25, Mark 13:1-37, and Luke 21:5-36. The language is metaphorical, and any attempt to interpret Jesus' words literally is in vain. The phrase "end of the world" should be translated "consummation" (Emphatic Diaglott). Jesus was not predicting the destruction of this planet. He was referring to the dissolution of an age of mortal thought and the ushering in of a new era of spiritual understanding.

When we read this discourse we should keep in mind that Jesus was speaking to His Apostles, the men who had been with Him as close companions during the three years of His ministry. They had at least some knowledge of the revolution in thought that results when a person applies Jesus' teaching. Those of us who are following Him in the regeneration know of the changes, often difficult, that take place with the passing of erroneous concepts and the coming of spiritual understanding. We should beware of false teachers who claim esoteric knowledge. We should wait in patience and faith for the Christ:

"Then if any one says to you, 'Lo, here is the Christ!' or 'There he is!' do not believe it. For false Christs and false prophets will arise and show great signs and wonders, so as to lead astray, if possible, even the elect. Lo, I have told you beforehand. So, if they say to you, 'Lo, he is in the wilderness,' do not go out; if they say, 'Lo, he is in the inner rooms,' do not believe it. For as the lightning comes from the east and shines as far as the west, so will be the coming of the Son of man" (Mt. 24:23-27).

Jesus enumerated various tests that will be met by spiritual aspirants. Even the "powers of the heavens will be shaken," i.e., their faith and understanding shall waver. Let them stand firm, for such a shaking will precede spiritual realization and be the sign of "the Son of man coming on the clouds of heaven" (Mt. 24:29-30).

"And then all the tribes of the earth will mourn, and they will see the Son of man coming on the clouds of heaven with power and great glory; and he will send out his angels with a loud trumpet call, and they will gather his elect from the four winds, from one end of heaven to the other" (Mt. 24:30-31).

There has been much diversity of opinion on the second coming of Christ. Unity believes that

Jesus' words should not be taken to mean that Jesus will again appear in the flesh. Had He not just said, "For as the lightning comes from the east and shines as far as the west, so will be the coming of the Son of man"? Surely the Christ, the Spirit of truth in humankind, will make Himself known to those who are spiritually quickened. To them, Christ is indeed a living presence "with power and great glory." Charles Fillmore states:

"The coming in the clouds of the heavens of the 'Son of man sitting on the right hand of Power' . . . is the 'second coming,' and we should look nowhere else for the advent of the risen Christ. Christ is today 'sitting at the right hand of Power,' which represents spiritual power expressed; the clouds of heaven being the obscurity in which sense consciousness holds the light of Truth.

"Let us cease expecting Christ to come in bodily form; let us turn our attention to His risen body already with us. In this way we shall cooperate with Him in setting up the kingdom of the heavens on the earth . . .

"The world needs the Christ consciousness. The need implies that the attainment is near at hand. There are men and women who gaze up into the heavens for Christ, as did the early disciples, instead of looking within their own heart and mind. 'Ye men of Galilee, why stand ye looking into heaven?' Only believe in the omnipresent Christ and you will behold Him sitting on the right hand of Power within your own being!'' (ASP 170-171)

Jesus pointed out that numerous obstacles will be encountered in the process of spiritual unfoldment. Yet He assures that these only indicate a greater degree of illumination in the future. When the branch of a fig tree becomes tender and puts forth leaves, then we know that summer is near (Mt. 24:32).

"Truly, I say to you, this generation will not pass away till all these things take place. Heaven and earth will pass away, but my words will not pass away. But of that day and hour no one knows, not even the angels of heaven, nor the Son, but the Father only. . . . Watch therefore, for you do not know on what day your Lord is coming" (Mt. 24:34-42).

Jesus continued the discourse with four parables on preparedness: the parable of the master and the thief (Mt. 24:43-44), the parable of the wise and evil servants (Mt. 24:45-51), the parable of the ten virgins (Mt. 25:1-13), and the parable of the talents (Mt. 25:14-30).

In the parable of the master and the thief, Jesus taught that we should always be on the alert to protect our spiritual consciousness (treasure). The mind of sense (thief) would steal or deprive us of faith, love, and wisdom. We should be in a spiritual consciousness at all times, "for the Son of man is coming at an hour you do not expect" (Mt. 24:44).

The parable of the wise and evil servants shows that our Lord has put us in charge of our being (His household) with instructions to tend and care for mind and body (our fellow servants). If enticements from the sense mind (evil servant) keep us from discharging our obligations, the law of God (Lord) will bring disaster to us, and "there men will weep and gnash their teeth" (Mt. 24:51).

One of the most familiar parables is that of the ten virgins. They represent aspirants to spiritual wisdom and power (waited for the bridegroom). Five were wise. They had attained sufficient understanding to raise their senses to a spiritual level (had oil in their lamps) and were prepared for a greater illumination. The five foolish virgins had not gained the necessary knowledge or spiritualized their senses (had no oil in their lamps). When the time for illumination was at hand (the bridegroom arrived), the wise virgins received the joy and power that Christ gives (attended the wedding feast). The foolish virgins had to take time to procure the required understanding and to train their senses (go and buy oil) and were not on hand when the summons came to enter the new life. "Watch therefore, for you know neither the day nor the hour" (Mt. 25:13).

The parable of the talents is somewhat similar to the parable of the pounds, given earlier in Jesus' ministry. The Lord gives spiritual gifts (talents) to all of us. If these are used rightly they increase, and we receive additional blessings. "Well done, good and faithful servant; you have been faithful over a little, I will set you over much; enter into the joy of your master" (Mt. 25:21). When we fail to use our God-given abilities (hide our talents) through fear or neglect, the law (Lord) demands an accounting. The inevitable result is that we are deprived of what has been given to us. "And cast the worthless servant into the outer darkness'' (Mt. 25:30).

Jesus concluded the Olivet Discourse with the parable of the sheep and goats (Mt. 25:31-46). This parable portrays the action of man as he begins to realize his divine sonship (''when the Son of man comes in his glory''). Our work now is to separate the true spiritual thoughts from the unredeemed vicious ones, even as a shepherd separates the sheep from the goats:

''Then the King will say to those at his right hand, 'Come, O blessed of my Father, inherit the kingdom prepared for you from the foundation of the world; for I was hungry and you gave me food, I was thirsty and you gave me drink, I was a stranger and you welcomed me, I was naked and you clothed me, I was sick and you visited me, I was in prison and you came to me.' Then the righteous will answer him, ''Lord, when did we see thee hungry and feed thee, or thirsty and give thee drink? And when did we see thee a stranger and welcome thee, or naked and clothe thee? And when did we see thee sick or in prison and visit thee?' And the King will answer them, 'Truly, I say to you, as you did it to one of the least of these my brethren, you did it to me.' Then he will say to those at his left hand,

'Depart from me, you cursed, into the eternal
fire prepared for the devil and his angels; for I
was hungry and you gave me no food, I was
thirsty and you gave me no drink, I was a
stranger and you did not welcome me, naked
and you did not clothe me, sick and in prison
and you did not visit me.' Then they also will
answer, 'Lord, when did we see thee hungry or
thirsty or a stranger or naked or sick or in prison,
and did not minister to thee?' Then he will
answer them, 'Truly, I say to you, as you did it
not to one of the least of these, you did it not to
me.' And they will go away into eternal punishment, but the righteous into eternal life'' (Mt.
25:34-46).

The King may be likened to the Christ, the I
AM which approves of our spiritual ideas and
promises us all good, but condemns unworthy
thoughts and warns us of trials ahead if we in-
dulge in negative thinking. There is nothing to
fear in this judgment if we preserve our divine
ideas and deny error thoughts:

''We are carried along by these thoughts [all
types of thoughts] until we reach the consciousness of our I AM power. We do not know

we are building ourselves, our environment, our world, until we reach this consciousness. Then judgment of our world begins and is passed on our thought creations. Suppose we have tried to cast the beam out of our eye so that we might help our brother. This act will answer in our judgment day. 'I was that "least" one.' . . .

"All things are in the consciousness and you have to learn to separate the erroneous from the true, darkness from light. The I AM must separate the sheep from the goats. This sifting begins right now and goes on until the perfect child of God is manifest and you are fully rounded out in all your Godlike attributes" (ASP 48-49).

On Tuesday evening, as Jesus and the Apostles walked toward Bethany in the twilight, He again reminded them of His coming trial: "You know that after two days the Passover is coming, and the Son of man will be delivered up to be crucified" (Mt. 26:2).

The events of this day, when Jesus had so completely baffled His opponents, led to a meeting of the Sanhedrin that night. The consensus of this meeting was that Jesus must be taken in secret, but that His capture should wait until after the Passover to prevent an uprising among the people in His behalf.

While the meeting in Jerusalem was going on,
Jesus reached Bethany:

"There they made him a supper; Martha
served, and Lazarus was one of those at table
with him. Mary took a pound of costly ointment
of pure nard and anointed the feet of Jesus and
wiped his feet with her hair; and the house was
filled with the fragrance of the ointment" (Jn.
12:2-3).

Judas objected to this, for he considered it a
waste, and asked, "Why was this ointment not
sold for three hundred denarii and given to the
poor?" (Jn. 12:5) Jesus replied, "Let her keep it
for the day of my burial. The poor you always
have with you, but you do not always have me"
(Jn. 12:7-8).

Mary represents the devotional aspect of humanity, which is filled with love for the Christ.
The anointing of Jesus' feet symbolizes the willingness of love to serve. Judas typifies the sense
thought, which is filled with selfishness.

"The Judas consciousness believes in poverty
and has no understanding of the true law of

supply. All that comes into consciousness is self-ishly appropriated and dissipated by this thief, yet he produces nothing'' (MJ 116).

Jesus' words, ''The poor you always have with you, but you do not always have me,'' mean that our service to the downtrodden is laudable, but there are likewise times when an expression of love should be given to our Lord. We are not always aware of Him (''you do not always have me'') but when we are aware of Him, the precious ointment of our devotion should be freely spent on Him. If we have a true prosperity consciousness, we know that one type of giving need not curtail us in any other form of helpfulness.

What motive prompted Judas to bargain with the Jews to betray Jesus? Perhaps he was stung by the Master's rebuke. Perhaps Judas felt that Jesus' cause was now lost and that he should salvage what he could from three years of following the Galilean. Or perhaps Judas thought that the betrayal would bring matters to a climax and force Jesus to declare Himself to be the Messiah. Whatever the motive, Judas went to Jerusalem that very night, sought out the Jewish authorities, and asked what they would pay him to deliver Jesus to them. They offered him thirty pieces of silver, the price of the meanest slave, and Judas agreed. Metaphysically,

"Judas represents the unredeemed life-forces. He also typifies that in humanity which, though it has caught the higher vision of life, still resorts to underhanded methods in order to meet its obligations. . . .

"Judas also symbolizes desire, appropriation, acquisitiveness. Acquisitiveness is a legitimate faculty of the mind, but covetousness is its Judas. When acquisitiveness acts within the law it builds up the consciousness. Exercised in its native realm, the free essences of Being, it draws to us the supplies of the universe and through it we enter into permanent possessions. But when it oversteps the law it is a destroyer. . . .

"And so we find among our disciples, or faculties, this one whose tendency is such that through it we are brought into condemnation and suffering. It is known from the first; it is Judas, self-appropriation. . . . It is through the exercising of this faculty that suffering and crucifixion are brought about. It is the faculty that draws to us the substance of things. While in its essence it is good, yet if one appropriates it in its personal sense 'good were it for that man if he had not been born.' . . .

"Judas is transformed and redeemed when all pertaining to personality is surrendered and the substance of divine love is poured into consciousness. Man is continually enriched as he gives up the things of sense and consecrates himself to purity of purpose" (MD 375-376).

After the intense activity of Sunday, Monday, and Tuesday, Jesus apparently remained in Bethany on Wednesday. Nothing is known of His activity on this day. Undoubtedly He spent it in prayer, preparing for the crucial test that He knew He was soon to meet.

CHAPTER XII

The Last Supper and Gethsemane

On Thursday, the day before the beginning of the Feast of the Passover, Jesus ate the paschal meal with His Apostles. To partake of this meal had long been the custom of the Jews.

The word *paschal* means "pertaining to the Passover," and refers especially to the paschal lamb that was slain by the priests and brought from the Temple to be roasted. The lamb was the main dish of the meal. The other food requirements were unleavened bread, wine, water, bitter herbs, and a sauce called charoseth. This meal, preceding the Feast of the Passover, carried out the ideas of sacrifice and redemption, and was eaten in remembrance of the lamb that was slain to protect the Israelites from the scourge of death at the time of their liberation from Egyptian bondage (Ex. 12). Jesus is frequently referred to as the Paschal Lamb. This is because He gave His life for the redemption of mankind.

On the day of the paschal meal the Apostles asked Jesus where the preparations were to be made for this meal. Selecting Peter and John,

Jesus asked them to go to Jerusalem.

"Behold, when you have entered the city, a man carrying a jar of water will meet you; follow him into the house which he enters, and tell the householder, 'The Teacher says to you, Where is the guest room, where I am to eat the passover with my disciples?' And he will show you a large upper room furnished; there make ready" (Lk. 22:10-12).

This was the last meal that Jesus ate with the Twelve before the Crucifixion, and it has come to be known as the Last Supper. In all probability it took place in the home of the parents of John Mark. This home served as a rendezvous for the disciples after the Crucifixion, and it was here that the Holy Spirit came to them on the day of Pentecost. Spiritually, the upper room signifies "the high state of mind that we assume in thinking about spiritual things. It may be attained through prayer, or by going into the silence with true words, or in spiritual meditation" (MD 668).

After Peter and John had made the proper preparations for the Supper they returned to Bethany. In the evening Jesus and the Twelve arrived at the house in Jerusalem and retired to the upper room. In his book, *The Life of Christ*, Frederick W. Farrar presents an interesting view of the scene:

"When they arrived the meal was ready, the table spread, the triclinia [mats] laid with cushions for the guests. Imagination loves to reproduce all the probable details of that deeply moving and eternally sacred scene, and if we compare the notices of ancient Jewish custom, with the immemorial fashions still existing in the changeless East, we can feel but little doubt as to the general nature of the arrangements. They were totally unlike those with which the genius of Leonardo da Vinci and other great painters has made us so familiar. The room probably had white walls, and was bare of all except the most necessary furniture and adornment. The couches or cushions, each large enough to hold three persons, were placed around three sides of one or more low tables of gaily painted wood, each scarcely higher than stools. The seat of honor was the central one of the central triclinium or mat. This was, of course, occupied by the Lord. . . . At the right hand of Jesus reclined the beloved disciple [John], whose head therefore could, at any moment, be placed upon the breast of his friend and Lord.''

As Jesus and the Apostles took their places there arose contention among the Twelve, probably as regards the seating arrangements. Jesus reminded them of their true position, saying:

"The kings of the Gentiles exercise lordship over them; and those in authority over them are called benefactors. But not so with you; rather let the greatest among you become as the youngest, and the leader as one who serves. . . . I am among you as one who serves'' (Lk. 22:25-27).

"And during supper . . . Jesus, knowing that the Father had given all things into his hands, and that he had come from God and was going to God, rose from supper, laid aside his garments, and girded himself with a towel'' (Jn. 13:2-4).

Then He washed the feet of the Apostles. It was the custom in those days for a person entering a house to take off his sandals so as not to bring in dust or dirt from the road. The Apostles had done this, but they had neglected to wash their feet. Generally the host had a servant perform this service for guests. As Jesus continued this menial task, awe and shame silenced the Apostles, until Jesus came to Peter, who protested:

" 'You shall never wash my feet.' Jesus answered him, 'If I do not wash you, you have no part in me.' Simon Peter said to him, 'Lord, not my feet only but also my hands and my head!' Jesus said to him, 'He who has bathed does not need to wash, except for his feet, but he is clean all over; and you are clean, but not every one of you.' For he knew who was to betray him; that was why he said, 'You are not all clean. . . . Do you know what I have done to you? You call me Teacher and Lord; and you are right, for so I am. If I then, your Lord and Teacher, have washed your feet, you also ought to wash one another's feet. . . . Truly, truly, I say to you, a servant is not greater than his master; nor is he who is sent greater than he who sent him. If you know these things, blessed are you if you do them' " (Jn. 13:8-17).

Peter's attitude of self-abnegation would serve to keep him from union with Spirit. The Christ always serves, and we cannot be too proud in the personal consciousness to refuse to accept His service. Jesus said, "If I do not wash you, you have no part in me." Peter comprehended something of the depth of Jesus' meaning when he made his plea, "Lord, not my feet only but also my hands and my head!" This was not necessary, for Jesus knew that Peter had begun the regeneration, and his understanding (represented by the feet) needed additional cleansing. The symbolic meaning of washing another's feet is that, as Jesus' followers, it is our duty to serve others by helping them to cleanse their consciousness of false beliefs and thus bring to them the light of true understanding.

As Jesus resumed the meal He was "troubled in spirit" and said, "One of you will betray me" (Jn. 13:21). The Apostles did not know of whom He spoke, and Peter leaned over and asked John to find out. John was reclining on the couch next to Jesus with his head on Jesus' breast. "Lord, who is it?" he inquired. Jesus answered:

" 'It is he to whom I shall give this morsel when I have dipped it.' So when he had dipped the morsel, he gave it to Judas, the son of Simon Iscariot" (Jn. 13:26).

Handing a sop to someone was not unusual, for at Eastern meals the guests ate out of a common bowl. A guest would dip a piece of bread into the bowl, take up a portion of meat, and then pass it to another guest. Judas, however, understood Jesus' action, and then "Satan entered into him." Jesus said to Judas, "What you are going to do, do quickly" (Jn. 13:27), and Judas, in haste, left the room. The other Apostles did not understand what Jesus said to John, and they thought that the Master had sent Judas on an errand.

Then Jesus said:

"Now is the Son of man glorified, and in him God is glorified . . . . Little children, yet a little while I am with you. You will seek me; and as I said to the Jews so now I say to you, 'Where I am going you cannot come.' A new commandment I give to you, that you love one another . . . . By this all men will know that you are my disciples, if you have love for one another" (Jn. 13:31-35).

Peter insisted on knowing where Jesus would go. When Jesus replied that Peter could not accompany Him now but would follow Him later, Peter asked, "Lord, why cannot I follow you now? I will lay down my life for you'' (Jn. 13:37). Peter represents faith, and faith is very sure of itself at times. But Jesus knew that faith, until it is made completely steadfast by spiritual realization, is changeable. He warned His loving yet fickle follower: "The cock will not crow, till you have denied me three times" (Jn. 13:38).

"Now as they were eating, Jesus took bread, and blessed, and broke it, and gave it to the disciples and said, 'Take, eat; this is my body.' And he took a cup, and when he had given thanks he gave it to them, saying, 'Drink of it, all of you; for this is my blood of the covenant, which is poured out for many for the forgiveness of sins'' (Mt. 26:26-28).

In The Gospel According to Luke these words are added: "Do this in remembrance of me" (Lk. 22:19). The Holy Communion has become a sacrament of the Christian church. Unity teaches that the bread represents divine substance and that the wine represents divine life. We are to eat and drink these; that is, we are to appropriate the substance of life of Christ through affirmative prayer: *Through Christ I now partake of divine substance. Through Christ*

I now partake of divine life. When we con-
template the divine ideas of substance and life,
our consciousness is charged with them and we
assimilate them. The result is the lifting of the
soul to a spiritual level. Unity does not believe
that communion is an act performed only in
church on Sunday, and it does not use the symbols of bread and wine. Unity holds that true
communion may be entered into when we turn
our attention to Christ and declare His substance
and life active in us now. Communion is the
form of prayer in which we seek at-one-ment
with Christ. Charles Fillmore states:

"The Christ substance (body) and the Christ
life (blood) are accessible at all times and in all
places to the one who awakens his I AM to spiritual omnipresence. The table of the Lord is
spread everywhere for those who believe on Him
as Spirit and in their Spirit affirmation eat of His
body and blood. The appropriation by His followers of His life and substance is the very foundation of salvation through Jesus Christ. The
mere acceptance intellectually of the teaching
that we are saved by the blood of the Lord Jesus
and the partaking of the bread and wine in a per-
functory manner will save neither mind nor

body. The only thing that will do it is the understanding that Jesus raised His body life and substance out of the race consciousness into Spirit consciousness and that with our mind poised in that consciousness we can lay hold of the Spirit elements that will save us to the uttermost" (JC 158-159).

While He was still in the upper room Jesus spoke the comforting words recorded in the 14th chapter of John. He knew the Apostles would have trials to meet after He had left them and He said:

"Let not your hearts be troubled; believe in God, believe also in me. In my Father's house are many rooms; if it were not so, would I have told you that I go to prepare a place for you? And when I go and prepare a place for you, I will come again and will take you to myself, that where I am you may be also" (Jn. 14:1-3).

Even as we believe in God, we should also believe in the Christ, God's manifestation in us. When we do, human anxiety passes. "Many rooms" means many abiding places. "The meaning of Jesus was that He was making a per-

manent abiding place for those who believed in
His teaching and accepted Him for what He
really was—God manifest. . . . The permanent
abiding place to which Jesus invited His friends
is 'prepared' by Him: He makes the place Himself; in fact, He is the place" (MJ 130). We may
always abide where He is by acknowledging His
presence.

"And you know the way where I am going"
(Jn. 14:4). Thomas protested that the Apostles
knew neither where Jesus was going nor the way.
"I am the way, and the truth, and the life; no
one comes to the Father, but by me," said Jesus
(Jn. 14:6). There is only one way to spiritual
realization (the Father) and that way is through
obedience to the Jesus Christ teaching. Then
Philip asked that the Apostles be shown the
Father, and Jesus answered:

"Have I been with you so long, and yet you do
not know me, Philip? He who has seen me has
seen the Father. . . . Do you not believe that I
am in the Father and the Father in me? The
words that I say to you I do not speak on my own
authority; but the Father who dwells in me does
his works" (Jn. 14:9-10).

When we come into an understanding of our spiritual nature, our oneness with the omnipresent principle of life, the Father is revealed.

"The Father principle may be so developed in man that it will move him unerringly in all his ways, and the Father may even speak words through his mouth. When this point is reached the question of man's unity with the Father principle is wholly removed, the manifestation of wisdom and power in him proving that a higher principle is at work through him" (MJ 131).

"Truly, truly, I say to you, he who believes in me will also do the works that I do; and greater works than these will he do, because I go to the Father. Whatever you ask in my name, I will do it, that the Father may be glorified in the Son; if you ask anything in my name, I will do it" (Jn. 14:12-14).

When, through faith, we have made union with the Christ mind, we shall be able to do the works that Jesus performed, and even "greater works." We shall be granted "whatever you ask in my name." His name stands for spiritual man (Christ), and to ask in the realization of the in-

dwelling Christ is to open our consciousness to
the infinite good that is resident in Spirit. Persons have asked in His name in a literal sense and
have not received. Prayer must be substantiated
by spiritual realization if we are to have the
fulfillment of the promise.

"If you love me, you will keep my commandments. And I will pray the Father, and he will
give you another Counselor, to be with you for
ever, even the Spirit of truth, whom the world
cannot receive, because it neither sees him nor
knows him; you know him, for he dwells with
you, and will be in you. I will not leave you
desolate; I will come to you. Yet a little while,
and the world will see me no more, but you will
see me; because I live, you will live also. In that
day you will know that I am in my Father, and
you in me, and I in you. He who has my commandments and keeps them, he it is who loves
me; and he who loves me will be loved by my
Father, and I will love him and manifest myself
to him" (Jn. 14:15-21).

Charles Fillmore's interpretation of these
verses is:

"In this Scripture Jesus, representing the I AM, gives assurance of divine co-operation to those who are loyal in thought and word to the Truth. You now know the relation in which you stand to the Father. Spiritually you are one, but to sustain this spiritual relation until it is fully manifested in your body and environment requires attention. The concrete aspect of Truth, represented by the personality of Jesus, must be taken away before you can understand Truth in its abstract or universal sense. Then withdrawing your attention from the letter or personality and centering it on Truth in its spiritual essence, you find that there is an intelligible side to that which seems vague and indefinite. The Comforter [Counselor], the Advocate, the Spirit of truth is omnipresent as divine wisdom and power, which are brought into active touch with our consciousness through our believing in Him. In 'the world'—on the phenomenal side—we cannot know this guide and helper, but having learned the truth about the omnipresence of Spirit, with all the abundance of life, love, Truth, and intelligence through which it is made manifest, we at once begin to realize that the Mighty One dwells with us, and 'shall be in you' " (MJ 133-134).

Continuing His discourse Jesus said: "These things I have spoken to you, while I am still with you. But the Counselor, the Holy Spirit, whom the Father will send in my name, he will teach you all things, and bring to your remembrance all that I have said to you" (Jn. 14:25-26).

Unity believes in the Trinity of Father, Son, and Holy Spirit, and interprets the Father as Principle, or God. The Son is the expression of God in the individual, namely, the Christ, or I AM. The Holy Spirit is called the Counselor or the Spirit of truth. Charles Fillmore says: "The Holy Spirit is neither the all of Being nor the fullness of Christ, but is an emanation, or breath, sent forth to do a definite work." The Holy Spirit is perhaps best understood as the "executive power of both Father and Son, carrying out the creative plan" (TT 134).

"Peace I leave with you; my peace I give to you; not as the world gives do I give to you. Let not your hearts be troubled, neither let them be afraid. . . . Rise, let us go hence" (Jn. 14:27, 31).

With this beautiful benediction ringing in their ears the Apostles silently followed Jesus from the room. While they walked along the road toward the garden of Gethsemane, Jesus told them of the need for a closer union with Him if they were to bring forth spiritual fruits. He clothed His lesson in the allegory of the vine and the branches:

"I am the true vine, and my Father is the vinedresser. Every branch of mine that bears no fruit, he takes away, and every branch that does bear fruit he prunes, that it may bear more fruit. You are already made clean by the word which I have spoken to you. Abide in me, and I in you. As the branch cannot bear fruit by itself, unless it abides in the vine, neither can you, unless you abide in me. . . . He who abides in me, and I in him, he it is that bears much fruit, for apart from me you can do nothing" (Jn. 15:1-5).

When we attempt to live without recognizing our dependence on the indwelling Christ, we are like a branch severed from the vine and receiving no nourishment. Charles Fillmore says:

"When our faith attaches itself to outer things, instead of the spiritual I AM, it ceases to draw vitality from the one and only source of all life, divine Principle. The only door to this life is the I AM. This abiding is a conscious centering of the mind in the depths within us by means of repeated affirmations of our faith and trust in it. This day-by-day repeating of affirmations finally opens a channel of intelligent communication with the silent forces at the depths of Being, thoughts and words flow forth from there, and an entirely new source of power is developed in the man'' (MJ 138-139).

In concluding this particular teaching Jesus reminded the Apostles that even as the Father loved Him, so He in turn loved them: "Abide in my love. . . . These things I have spoken to you, that my joy may be in you, and that your joy may be full. This is my commandment, that you love one another as I have loved you" (Jn. 15:9-12).

It is not difficult for us to abide in Jesus when we love Him and know that He loves us. As we abide in Him, we may feel His joy and appropriate it for ourselves. Then we can obey what is sometimes referred to as the eleventh commandment, namely, that we love one another "as I have loved you."

Jesus warned the Apostles of persecutions that would come. "If they persecuted me, they will

persecute you'' (Jn. 15:20). He urged them to
remember what He had said. It was expedient
for Him to leave them, ''for if I do not go away,
the Counselor will not come to you; but if I go, I
will send him to you'' (Jn. 16:7). So long as we
depend on a person, no matter how spiritual he
may be, we do not find the Spirit of truth
(Counselor) within ourselves. Each of us must
make his or her own spiritual demonstration and
should not lean on anyone, even on Jesus as a
man. We find our own Christ self by adhering to
Jesus' teaching and it is then we realize that the
spiritual presence of Jesus has been with us all
the time, and that without Him our search
would have been fruitless.

The Apostles did not understand Jesus' prediction: ''A little while, and you will see me no
more; again a little while, and you will see me''
(Jn. 16:16). He was referring to the Crucifixion
and the Resurrection. The first would separate
Him from them, and the second would bring
Him back to them. However, they did realize
that some great change was about to take place
when He said, ''I came from the Father and have
come into the world; again, I am leaving the
world and going to the Father'' (Jn. 16:28). Jesus
had no fear of coming events, for He knew that it

was in His power to overcome anything the world could inflict on Him.

As Jesus and the Apostles drew near Gethsemane, Jesus lifted up His eyes and prayed what is known as the Prayer of Intercession. There are three distinct parts to the prayer: the first part for Himself, the second for the Apostles, and the third for future believers:

"Father, the hour has come; glorify thy Son that the Son may glorify thee, since thou hast given him power over all flesh, to give eternal life to all whom thou hast given him. And this is eternal life, that they know thee the only true God, and Jesus Christ whom thou hast sent. I glorified thee on earth, having accomplished the work which thou gavest me to do; and now, Father, glorify thou me in thy own presence with the glory which I had with thee before the world was made" (Jn. 17:1-5).

Charles Fillmore states:

"In this Scripture Jesus was asking of the Father as never before. To glorify means to magnify with praise, to enhance with spiritual splendor, to adorn. Jesus was asking for a full and complete unification of His consciousness with that of the Father. Jesus realized that He had been given all authority over the flesh. He was holding the realization not only for His own glorification but also for that of His disciples. Jesus realized that in this union a full understanding of God and His laws would be revealed, which would naturally make clear to Him the way of eternal life'' (MJ 147).

In praying that He would be glorified with the glory that He had had with the Father ''before the world was made,'' Jesus was recognizing the Christ as eternal and existing in full consciousness of wholeness before there had been a manifest world.

His prayer for the Apostles was made in the realization that the Father had given them to Him to instruct in His word, and ''they have kept thy word'' (Jn. 17:6). ''Holy Father, keep them in thy name, which thou hast given me, that they may be one, even as we are one'' (Jn. 17:11). While with them He had instructed the Apostles in spiritual things, and they were lifted above worldly thoughts. Now He prayed not that they be taken from the world, but that they be preserved from the ''evil one'' (worldly consciousness). "Sanctify them in the truth; thy word is truth. As thou didst send me into the world, so I have sent them into the world" (Jn. 17:17-18).

The third and last portion of the Prayer of Intercession was for those who "believe in me through their word" (Jn. 17:20). He asked that they, too, be able to recognize their oneness with the Father and with Him, "even as thou, Father, art in me, and I in thee, that they also may be in us, so that the world may believe that thou hast sent me" (Jn. 17:21). Through them God's Word was to be given to many, and Jesus prayed "that the love with which thou hast loved me may be in them, and I in them" (Jn. 17:26).

"In proportion as people understand and have faith in Jesus as their actual Savior from sin, and in proportion as they are set free from appetite, passion, jealousy, prejudice, and all selfishness, they experience wholeness of mind and body as the result. The ultimate result of this knowledge and of daily practice in overcoming (even as Jesus Himself overcame) will be a new race that will demonstrate eternal life—the lifting up of the whole man—spirit, soul, and body—into the Christ consciousness of oneness with the Father.

This is indeed true glorification. By means of the reconciliation, glorification, and at-one-ment that Jesus Christ re-established between God and man we can regain our original estate as sons of God here upon earth" (MJ 149).

The tones of this intercessory prayer faded away, and Jesus and the Eleven arrived at the garden of Gethsemane. At the gate He stopped and motioned to Peter, James, and John to accompany Him. He bade the others, ''Sit here, while I go yonder and pray'' (Mt. 26:36). As He and the three moved away He said to them, ''My soul is very sorrowful, even to death; remain here, and watch with me'' (Mt. 26:38). Alone, He went farther into the garden and there He fell on the ground, praying, ''My Father, if it be possible, let this cup pass from me; nevertheless, not as I will, but as thou wilt'' (Mt. 26:39).

Many people believe that the will of God for all is health, abundance, peace, and joy. When these things are not in evidence, it is right to pray for them. However, the greatest prayer that anyone can utter is ''not as I will, but as thou wilt.'' There comes a time to each of us in our spiritual ongoing when the lesser good should be overshadowed by the greater. Our goal is noth-

ing less than the realization of complete oneness
with God. This is Christ mastery. We may shrink
from what appears to be a difficult test, and we
may cry, "Let this cup pass from me," but our
surrender to God's will is all that is necessary to
ensure the outworking of His good.

After His prayer Jesus returned to the three
Apostles and found them sleeping. "So, could
you not watch with me one hour? Watch and
pray that you may not enter into temptation; the
spirit indeed is willing, but the flesh is weak"
(Mt. 26:40-41). Twice more Jesus prayed the
same prayer. Twice more He returned to find the
Apostles sleeping. After the third time He was
completely at peace. Looking again on the slum-
bering men, He said:

"Are you still sleeping and taking your rest?
Behold, the hour is at hand, and the Son of man
is betrayed into the hands of sinners. Rise, let us
be going; see, my betrayer is at hand" (Mt.
26:45-46).

Jesus' praying in the garden represents:

"The struggle that takes place within the consciousness when Truth is realized as the one reali-

ty. All the good is pressed out and saved and the error is denied away. This is often agony—the suffering that the soul undergoes in giving up its cherished idols or in letting go of human consciousness.

"The great work of everyone is to incorporate the Christ mind in soul and body. The process of eliminating the old consciousness and entering into the new may be compared to Gethsemane, whose meaning is *oil press* . . . a press is an emblem of trial, distress, agony, while oil points to Spirit and illumination" (MD 321).

Several hours had passed since Judas left the upper room where the Last Supper was held. He had gone to the high priest and had indicated that this was the time to turn Jesus over to the Jews. The high priest gave Judas an escort of armed men, and Judas, knowing where Jesus was likely to be, led them to the garden of Gethsemane. He gave his companions a sign, saying, "The one I shall kiss is the man; seize him and lead him away under guard" (Mk. 14:44). On approaching Jesus, Judas greeted Him and kissed Him.

Jesus knew that He would be betrayed, but He made no effort to defeat the act of Judas. Sense consciousness betrays us every day, yet it would be unwise to destroy it before its time, because at its foundation it is good. We are continually enriched as we give up the things of sense and consecrate ourselves to purity of purpose.

Defense seemed useless, especially as Jesus made no effort to save Himself, and the Apostles stood helplessly by; that is, all but Peter. Peter, the impulsive, drew a sword and severed the ear of Malchus, a servant of the high priest. Instantly Jesus rebuked Peter:

"Put your sword back into its place; for all who take the sword will perish by the sword. Do you think that I cannot appeal to my Father, and he will at once send me more than twelve legions of angels?" (Mt. 26:52-53)

Jesus then touched the ear of Malchus and it was healed. Malchus, the high priest's servant, symbolizes the limited understanding and judgment of the ruling power that the high priest represents. Peter's cutting off Malchus' right ear may be interpreted as meaning that we should not use our faith destructively. Such a proceeding would only serve to further limit the possibilities of a person's perceiving and laying hold of Truth. Jesus' healing the ear shows that limited understanding and judgment should be healed, illumined, and lifted up instead of being pushed still farther into unreceptivity and darkness.

The men who had come with Judas to take Jesus had not known what to expect. When they saw that Jesus had no intention of resisting arrest, they seized and bound Him. No doubt the Apostles were overcome with surprise and distress upon being confronted by a multitude armed with "swords and clubs." "Then all the disciples forsook him and fled" (Mt. 26:56). Thus alone, Jesus was led a captive to the palace of the high priest, Caiaphas.

CHAPTER XIII

Trials and Crucifixion

After Jesus had been seized, bound, and placed in the custody of Jewish officials He was given two trials—one religious and the other civil. In each there were three stages. The religious trial consisted of His appearance before Annas, then before Caiaphas and an informal committee made up of members of the Sanhedrin, and last, an appearance before a regular meeting of this court. The civil trial took place first before Pontius Pilate; then before Herod Antipas, tetrarch of Galilee and Perea; and then again before Pilate. No one Gospel contains the full information about these trials, but by putting the various events in the four accounts together, the whole story is related.

The reason for this double legal procedure was that, although the Sanhedrin could try both civil and religious cases affecting the Jews, it could not give an order for the execution of a prisoner on whom it had passed the death sentence. Only the Roman procurator, Pontius Pilate, had this power. Therefore, when the Sanhedrin condemned Jesus to death, it had to ask Pilate to issue the order for crucifixion. Crucifixion was a Roman form of execution. If the Sanhedrin had been able to inflict the death penalty, Jesus would have been stoned.

Jesus was taken first to Annas. Annas had been the high priest before Caiaphas, his son-in-law, was appointed, and he still was the real power in the Sanhedrin. John 18:19-24 records the proceedings of the first stage of Jesus' trial, which began before dawn on Friday morning.

When Annas questioned Jesus about His teachings, Jesus said that He had preached openly in the synagogues and the Temple where the Jews came together, and that He never had taught in secret. He suggested that Annas question those who had heard Him preach as regards His teachings. Annas felt that this answer was disrespectful, and he sent Jesus to Caiaphas, who had hurriedly called together some of the members of the Sanhedrin. The account is reported in Matthew 26:59-68 and Mark 14:55-65. Two witnesses testified falsely against Jesus, saying that He had claimed superhuman power. Jesus did not answer the charges, and Caiaphas demanded:

" 'I adjure you by the living God, tell us if

you are the Christ, the Son of God.' Jesus said to him, 'You have said so. But I tell you, hereafter you will see the Son of man seated at the right hand of Power, and coming on the clouds of heaven' '' (Mt. 26:63-64).

Cries of ''blasphemy'' rang through the room, and the assembled Jews declared that He deserved to die.

While Jesus was appearing before Annas and Caiaphas, Peter and John came to the high priest's residence. John knew the high priest and gained admittance, but Peter was stopped at the door. In the court outside the residence, a group of servants were warming themselves by a fire of coals. Peter joined them, and at different times three persons asked if he were not the friend of the Galilean prisoner. Each time Peter denied that he knew Jesus. Just as the third denial left Peter's lips, Jesus was led across the court to the guardhouse to await the formal meeting of the Sanhedrin. Thus, Jesus heard His boldest apostle's repudiation of Him, and He looked straight at Peter. Immediately a cock crowed, and ''Peter remembered the saying of Jesus, 'Before the cock crows, you will deny me three times.' And he went out and wept bitterly'' (Mt. 26:75).

Peter's denial of Jesus shows us that while spiritual faith is being developed in consciousness it is often changeable and wavering:

"Until faith is thoroughly identified with the Christ, you will find that the Peter faculty in you is a regular weathercock. It will in all sincerity affirm its allegiance to Spirit, and then in the hour of adversity will deny that it even knew Spirit. This, however, is in its probationary period. When you have trained it to look to Christ for all things, under all circumstances, it becomes the staunchest defender of the faith" (MD 517).

According to Jewish law, a legal meeting of the Sanhedrin could not be held before sunrise, which would be about six o'clock. At that time, Jesus was led before the Sanhedrin, the supreme court of the Jews, the majority of whose members were determined that He should die. The account is recorded in Luke 22:66-71.

As in the formal trial before Caiaphas, only one charge was brought against Jesus—blasphemy. When asked if He was the Son of God, Jesus replied, " 'You say that I am.' And they said, 'What further testimony do we need? We have heard it ourselves from his own lips' " (Lk.

22:70-71). Their next action was to take Jesus to
Pilate with the request that He be executed.

The religious trial of Jesus "shows how a
merely formal religion will persecute and attempt to kill the inner Christ Spirit and all that
pertains to it" (MJ 154).

Doubtless Judas had kept himself posted on
all that occurred. When he heard the decision of
the Sanhedrin and knew that Pilate would be
asked to pronounce the death sentence, Judas
realized fully what he had done. Hastening to
the chief priests, he attempted to return the
thirty pieces of silver he had received for betraying Jesus, saying, "I have sinned in betraying innocent blood" (Mt. 27:4). The priests would not
take the money, and Judas, in an agony of re-
morse, threw down the silver in the sanctuary
and "went and hanged himself" (Mt. 27:5).

The death of Judas signifies the dissolution of
the unredeemed life-forces that betray us. It
makes way for the lifting up of the forces that
will aid us in laying hold of spiritual life. Matthias, whose name means "given wholly unto
Jehovah," was later selected to replace Judas as
an apostle.

The Jewish leaders took Jesus to Pilate. The
fullest account of the first appearance of these

leaders and Jesus before the Roman procurator is given in John 18:28-38. When Pilate asked the Jews what charge they preferred against the prisoner, they poured forth a volley of accusations. The chief one was that Jesus set Himself up as a king. The Sanhedrin had condemned Him for blasphemy, but such a charge would have been ignored by Pilate who cared nothing for the religion of the Jews. Therefore, a charge that would represent Jesus as a threat to the Roman government had to be invented.

Instead of condemning Jesus unheard, Pilate questioned Him privately: "Are you the King of the Jews?" he asked (Jn. 18:33). Jesus replied:

" 'My kingship is not of this world . . . . You say that I am a king. For this I was born, and for this I have come into the world, to bear witness to the truth. Every one who is of the truth hears my voice.' Pilate said to him, 'What is truth?' After he had said this, he went out to the Jews again, and told them, 'I find no crime in him' " (Jn. 18:36-38).

Pilate represents:

"The ruling principle of the sense plane,

the carnal will. Pilate questioned the I AM,
Jesus . . . 'Art thou the King of the Jews?' Ap-
plying this to the individual man, one would say
to oneself, 'Is there a ruling will over my religious nature?' The personal will has no concept
of the factors of that inner higher realm, and
believes that it is the ruler of the whole man. It is
jealous of any attempt to usurp its power, but
when it is assured that the kingdom that the
higher self would rule is 'not of this world,' it
finds in that self 'no fault' '' (MD 530).

The Jews greeted Pilate's verdict with anger
and insisted that Jesus was a disturber of the
peace. When he learned that Jesus was a Galilean, Pilate thought to rid himself of a troublesome case by sending Him to Herod Antipas,
tetrarch of Galilee, who was then in Jerusalem to
attend the Passover.

The account of Jesus' appearance before
Herod is given in Luke 23:6-12. Herod was
pleased to see Jesus, as he had heard many
reports of His miracles and wanted to witness
one. "So he [Herod] questioned him [Jesus] at
some length; but he made no answer" (Lk.
23:9). The Jews standing by continued to accuse
Jesus. Herod, evidently angered by Jesus' si-

lence, allowed the soldiers to mock Him and, in derision of His supposed kingly role, they arrayed Him in a gorgeous robe and sent Him back to Pilate. Herod passed no sentence on Jesus.

The third stage of the civil trial is recorded in each gospel. The most detailed account is given in John 18:39-40 and 19:1-16. Pilate's duty was to acquit Jesus, since he had turned the case over to Herod, tetrarch of the territory in which Jesus lived, and Herod had dismissed Him. Pilate tried to acquit Him by telling the Jews that neither he nor Herod had found Jesus guilty of any crime that was worthy of death. It was the custom for Rome to release a Jewish prisoner during the Passover, and Pilate suggested that Jesus be released. Pilate wanted to save an innocent man and at the same time appease the Jews, but they would not hear of it. "Not this man, but Barabbas!" (Jn. 18:40) they shouted. Barabbas was a robber and the leader of a recent revolt against Rome, yet the people chose to release him instead of Jesus. As a last resort, and hoping that the Jews' wrath might be satisfied by scourging Jesus, Pilate gave Him over to the Roman soldiers for scourging. After the soldiers had done this, in derision they placed a crown of thorns on His head, "and arrayed Him in a purple robe"

(Jn. 19:2), calling Him "King of the Jews!"

"Pilate went out again, and said to them, 'See, I am bringing him out to you, that you may know that I find no crime in him.' So Jesus came out, wearing the crown of thorns and the purple robe. Pilate said to them, 'Behold the man!' " (Jn. 19:4-5)

Perhaps Pilate's words, "Behold the man," implied that he thought Jesus' punishment had been sufficient and that he was returning the man they had brought to him. Or perhaps Pilate's words meant that he recognized the greatness of Jesus and in admiration acknowledged the Man among men.

However, the Jewish leaders, together with the rabble they had incited, cried, "Crucify him." When Pilate still demurred, the Jews brought up their real charge against Jesus—that He called Himself the Son of God. Again Pilate questioned Jesus, and again he wished to free Him. But the Jews, in desperation, said: "If you release this man, you are not Caesar's friend; every one who makes himself a king sets himself against Caesar" (Jn. 19:12). This was the subtle insinuation to Pilate that by protecting Jesus he was harboring a traitor to the Roman government. If such a report were relayed to Rome, it would undoubtedly cause serious trouble for Pilate and could even mean his death. He therefore gave the order for the crucifixion of Jesus, making it clear to the Jews that he considered himself "innocent of this man's blood" (Mt. 27:24).

The trial of Jesus, resulting in the Crucifixion, symbolizes a man who is controlled by human consciousness. Pilate gave the order under duress. The innate sense of justice that is present in all people was in the case of Pilate violated by the Jewish leaders' insistence that Jesus be executed. Pilate himself was not emotionally involved in the situation and, therefore, his finer instincts and his understanding had opportunity to assert themselves. The Jews, on the other hand, had what they considered a just case. The Pharisees hated Jesus because they considered Him a menace to their religion; the Sadducees wanted Him out of the way because they considered Him an agitator who threatened their political and economic security. Thus, both Jewish parties were emotionally involved, and their sense of justice was obscured. Their fault was spiritual blindness. Our attitude toward those who caused the crucifixion of Jesus should be one of compas-

sion rather than condemnation. The main points
of Jesus' teaching are that we love God and our
fellow human beings, but in order to do this a
certain degree of spiritual understanding and
development is necessary. As Christians we are
endeavoring to attain this spiritual level now by
releasing all criticism and prejudice and by striving to manifest the Christ virtues of forgiveness,
tolerance, and love.

After the Roman soldiers had again mocked
Jesus they stripped Him of the purple robe, put
on Him His own garments, and a Cross was laid
on His shoulders. According to the historian
Plutarch, it was customary for a criminal to carry
his cross to the place of execution. "Two others
also, who were criminals, were led away to be put
to death with him" (Lk. 23:32).

Golgotha (*Calvary* in its Latin form), a well-
known site just outside the gates of Jerusalem,
was selected as the place for the Crucifixion. The
word Golgotha means "a place of the skull,"
and Charles Fillmore states:

"The seat of the conscious mind is the front
brain, and there the will has established its dominion. There all things affecting the body are
either admitted or rejected. Even spiritual Truth

has to be admitted through this door before it can become part of the consciousness. It is there that the human will must be crossed out, to give the divine will free expression" (MD 240).

Jesus had come through a terrific ordeal, having been scourged, mocked, and buffeted by His accusers, and as the procession made its way toward Golgotha, He tottered under the weight of the Cross. Simon, a man of Cyrene who was bound for Jerusalem, was compelled by the soldiers to bear the Cross for Jesus.

Among the crowd that followed Jesus were many women who lamented His plight. Jesus admonished them not to weep for Him. No matter how severe the suffering is that comes to us, we should remember that we shall pass through the valley of the shadow in safety if we remain steadfast in faith. But Jesus made a stern prediction of impending disaster for the Jews. In days of distress they would long for death and "then they will begin to say to the mountains, 'Fall on us'; and to the hills, 'Cover us' '' (Lk. 23:30).

When the procession reached Golgotha, and before Jesus was put on the Cross, the Roman soldiers offered Him "wine mingled with myrrh" (Mk. 15:23). Crucifixion was the cruelest form of execution, and it was an evidence of compassion on the part of the executioners that they customarily gave those who were to be crucified a draught of wine medicated with a powerful narcotic to dull the excruciating pain. "But he [Jesus] did not take it" (Mk. 15:23). He chose to be in full control of all His faculties. The Crucifixion was to be the crucial moment of His life. He would meet it with the Father, of whose love and mercy He was confident.

On Friday morning at the "third hour" (nine o'clock) the crosses were raised. Jesus was in the middle, with a thief on each side. On a white wooden tablet above His head was written, in Latin, Greek, and Hebrew, "JESUS OF NAZARETH, THE KING OF THE JEWS." This was Pilate's way of inflicting public scorn on the Jews. Immediately, a committee called on Pilate with the request that the inscription be removed, but Pilate was adamant and said, "What I have written I have written" (Jn. 19:22).

The Roman soldiers stripped Jesus of His garments and divided them. However, when they saw His coat they agreed not to tear it but to cast lots for its possession. The coat, or seamless robe as it is generally called, was a beautiful and valuable garment "without seam, woven from top to bottom'' (Jn. 19:23). It represents:

"The truth in its harmonious expression and unchangeable perfection.

"Regeneration forms a new mind and a new body consciousness. . . . The seamless coat of Jesus symbolizes a consciousness of the indestructible unity of life and substance in the body consciousness. This consciousness inheres in the executive department of mind in man (soldiers), and can be exercised by Spirit in body projection when so desired" (MD 153).

The scene was one of tumult. Many of the watchers stood by silently. Some mocked Jesus, bidding Him come down from the Cross and save Himself. Likewise, the chief priests and scribes taunted, "He saved others; he cannot save himself" (Mk. 15:31).

The Crucifixion symbolizes the crossing out of all that belongs to the mortal consciousness in order that the way may be made for the coming forth of the Christ self. Jesus' seven last words (or sayings) on the Cross symbolize steps that should be taken in the final overcoming of the mortal mind.

No one gospel records all of Jesus' seven last

words. Each gives either one or three of them, and Bible scholars have arranged them in sequential order.

During the first three hours after Jesus was placed on the Cross He spoke three times. In these words He fulfilled His entire obligation to humankind: first, by forgiving His enemies; second, by promising mercy to the repentant sinner; and third, by discharging His responsibility to His mother.

"Father, forgive them; for they know not what they do" (Lk. 23:34).

This saying was addressed to His persecutors and reveals His forgiving love. Unforgiveness is a most destructive emotion, and it is based on a lack of understanding. Those who are unjust to us "know not what they do," for injustice breeds injustice for those who perpetrate it. We should pray for these people. By doing this we enter into the Christ forgiveness that cleanses us of the injustices we have committed unconsciously or deliberately.

"Today you will be with me in Paradise" (Lk. 23:43).

Jesus' Cross was between those of the two criminals. One of these taunted Him, "Are you not the Christ? Save yourself and us!" (Lk. 23:39) The other reprimanded him, saying that they indeed were receiving their just desert but that Jesus was an innocent man. Turning to Jesus, the repentant man said, "Remember me when you come into your kingdom" (Lk. 23:42), and Jesus made him the great promise, "Today you will be with me in Paradise." Whenever we turn to Christ, confess our sins, and ask His help, it is always freely given. Through His grace, we shall enter into paradise (consciousness of peace and wholeness).

"Woman, behold, your son! . . . Behold, your mother!" (Jn. 19:26-27)

Jesus addressed these words to Mary and the apostle John, who were standing near the Cross. Thus He fulfilled His responsibility to His mother, and tradition states that Mary lived with John for the remainder of her life. Jesus' action reminds us that it is our duty to provide for those who have a right to expect provision from us. To discharge our human responsibilities will- ingly and lovingly is a definite part of spiritual unfoldment.

Jesus was on the Cross for three more hours, from noon until shortly after three in the afternoon. During these hours there was "darkness over the whole land," and Jesus was silent until just before three o'clock. At that time He uttered a cry of desolation and physical anguish.

"My God, my God, why hast thou forsaken me?" (Mk. 15:34)

By giving expression to this universal sense of aloneness in trial Jesus released it for Himself and for us. Experiencing crucifixion spiritually, an erasing of all sense thought and feeling, is difficult when we face it. During this trying time we may feel that even God has forsaken us. When these periods of darkness and doubt come, we should remember that Jesus passed through a similar period. We should remember also that it was comparatively momentary for Him and will be for us. The challenge is to persevere until the demonstration is completed.

"I thirst" (Jn. 19:28).

This is the cry of the body and symbolizes

physical distress of every kind. There comes a time in spiritual unfoldment when we must know that the body is not limited to the physical. It is composed of divine substance and activated by divine intelligence. It is the temple of the Lord, and its full needs can be met only by drinking of the living water (the word of Christ). Jesus voiced the demand of the body for Himself and us, and we should remember that if we remain staunch in faith our body shall be lifted to spiritual perfection.

Near the Cross stood a jar that contained a sour wine (vinegar) from which the Roman soldiers had drunk. When Jesus said, "I thirst," one of them took a sponge and, filling it with the liquid, raised it to Jesus' lips. Jesus accepted this simple act of mercy. Almost immediately He spoke the words that revealed the heights to which His consciousness had risen.

"It is finished" (Jn. 19:30).

Jesus' suffering was now almost over. His work was finished. His mission was to show "the way, and the truth and the life," and this had now been accomplished. Henceforth for Him the limited kingdom of earth would be supplanted by the finished kingdom of God. When we undergo a severe trial and keep the faith, we finally come to the place of knowing that every vestige of human effort is exhausted. God is in control. Our release is very near. This release came to Jesus, and it will come to us when the seventh or last word is spoken:

"Father, into thy hands I commit my spirit!" (Lk. 23:46)

In complete surrender to the Father, Jesus' prayer, "not my will, but thine, be done," was answered. The life of Spirit was on the march, and victory was its only outcome. When we give ourselves fully to Him, the last barrier between the personal and the spiritual is dissolved. The way is open then for His action to take place in us, and He cannot fail.

When Jesus spoke this last word, He "gave up his spirit" (Jn. 19:30). At that moment the veil of the Temple was rent in two from the top to the bottom:

"The last step in regeneration is the giving up of the thought of the corporeal existence of the body temple. Then the veil of sense thought that conceals the spiritual body is rent, and man comes into consciousness of the body imperishable and eternal'' (MD 673).

An earthquake shook the earth and split the rocks, and even the Roman soldiers were no longer indifferent. In awe they exclaimed, "Truly this was the Son of God!" (Mt. 27:54)

"At the crucifixion of Jesus it was the human consciousness of a perishable body that died. 'Our old man was crucified with him, that the body of sin might be done away, that so we should no longer be in bondage to sin.' When the thoughts of sin and death are crossed out, the spiritual truth about life and its manifestation in the body takes form in consciousness'' (MD 348).

The Sabbath began at sunset on Friday, and the Jews wanted the bodies of the three men taken down from the crosses before that time. They went to Pilate with the request that the legs of the men be broken to hasten their deaths. The Roman soldiers did this to the two thieves, but when they came to Jesus they discovered that He was dead. To make absolutely sure, one of them drove a spear into His side.

Joseph of Arimathaea, a prominent Jew and a member of the Sanhedrin, and secretly a follower of Jesus, asked Pilate for Jesus' body for burial. The request was granted, and with the help of Nicodemus, Joseph wrapped the body in linen and laid it in a new tomb in his garden. A huge stone was then rolled to the entrance of the tomb. By the time the men had completed their ministrations it was sunset, and the Sabbath had begun.

The Crucifixion of Jesus became the foundation of the Christian doctrine of salvation by the blood of Jesus. Christians generally believe that Jesus gave His blood on the Cross as a sacrifice for the sins of every person, and that when one accepts Him as Savior one is saved by His blood. The Jews have always believed that sin was expiated through sacrifice and that the blood of the slain animal on the altar cleansed man of sin. Jesus has been considered the "sacrificial lamb" who was killed to bring about a reconciliation of sinful man to God.

Unity accepts this doctrine, but gives it a different interpretation. Unity believes that we are saved by appropriating His blood, which represents spiritual life. Charles Fillmore says:

"Jesus raised the blood of His body to spiritual potency. This purified blood was sown as seed in our race thought and can be appropriated by anyone who raises his thoughts to those of Jesus. This is accomplished through faith in Jesus to save one from sin, to inspire one with His Spirit, or through asking Jesus to come to the aid of the sin-sick mind or suffering body. A single atom of the purified blood of Jesus can begin a vitalizing and purifying work in mind and body that will continue until the Christ man appears" (KL 28).

The doctrine of the vicarious atonement is also associated with Jesus' crucifixion. Unity teaches that Jesus did indeed make an atonement for humankind, not by His death but by His life, His teaching, and His final overcoming of death. Prior to the ministry of Jesus humankind had been held in the bondage of limitation by erroneous beliefs and consequent sins:

"We can readily see how a whole race might be caught in the meshes of its own thought emanations and, through this drowsy ignorance of the man ego, remain there throughout eternity, unless a break were made in the structure and the light of a higher way let in. This is exactly what has happened to our race. In our journey back to the Father's house we became lost in our own thought emanations, and Jesus Christ broke through the crystallized thought strata and opened the way for all those who will follow Him.

"By so doing He made a connection between our state of consciousness and the more interior one of the Father—He united them—made them a unit—*one*, hence the at-one-ment or atonement through Him. He became the way by which all who accept Him may 'pass over' to the new consciousness. That which died upon the cross was the consciousness of all mortal beliefs that hold us in bondage—such as sin, evil, sickness, fleshly lusts, and death—which He overcame. 'I have overcome the world.' Jesus' 'overcoming' made a great rent in the sense consciousness, and opened a way by which all who desire may demonstrate easily and quickly" (TT 165-166).

In order for us to take advantage of the atonement Jesus made for us, it is imperative that we follow Him. "Keep my word," He said. This means that we are to take on His ideas, speak His word, and do the things that He did. He set an example and He showed that whatever He urged others to do He could do. He taught love by showing love. He taught forgiveness by forgiving those who despitefully used Him. He admonished, "Seek ye first his kingdom and his righteousness" and made that search the first consideration of His life. His is the greatest service ever rendered to humanity, for He released the Christ consciousness to the world. The only way we can unify ourselves with the Christ is:

"By centering our mind on Jesus and silently asking His help in our demonstrations. It is not the prayer of a 'worm of the dust' to a god, but of one who is on the way asking the guidance of one who has passed over the same road, and who knows all the hard places and how to get through them.

"This in one sense is the relation of Jesus Christ to each of us, and so far as our present demonstration is concerned, it is the most important relation. The road that we are traveling from the mortal plane of consciousness to the spiritual plane is beset with many obstructions, and we need the assistance of one stronger than any of those who now dwell in flesh bodies. He who is still in the perception of the earthly is not always a safe guide, because he sees in a limited way. We want one who sees wholly in Spirit, and such a one we find in Jesus Christ'' (TT 168-169).

CHAPTER XIV

Resurrection, Appearances, and Ascension

The Jewish Sabbath that immediately preceded the Resurrection in A.D. 30 must have been a time of stress and strain for the followers of Jesus. No record can be found of the whereabouts of the Apostles during this time, but several of the women who had stood at the Cross saw where Jesus had been laid. They watched at the tomb until the Sabbath began. Then they retired to their homes for rest, in accordance with the Jewish custom.

Shortly after the Crucifixion the chief priests went to Pilate and insisted that Jesus' tomb be guarded for three days. They recalled the rumored prophecies of His resurrection and were afraid that His disciples would steal the body and spread abroad the report that Jesus had risen from the dead. Pilate granted their request. The tomb was sealed, and a Roman guard was left to watch it.

Within the tomb, man's greatest overcoming was taking place.

"The three days that Jesus was in the tomb represent the three movements of mind that are involved in overcoming error. First, nonresistance and humility; second, the taking on of the divine activity, or receiving the will of God; third, the assimilation and fulfillment of the divine will" (MD 349).

Jesus had already accomplished the demonstration over the last enemy, death, when, at dawn on the first day of the week, Mary Magdalene, Mary the mother of James, and Salome hastened toward the sepulcher. They had prepared spices and ointments to anoint Jesus' body, and as they approached the garden where Jesus was buried, they wondered, "Who will roll away the stone for us from the door of the tomb?" (Mk. 16:3) The women did not know that the tomb had been sealed and guarded. They did not know that there had been an earthquake and that the stone no longer barred the entrance to the tomb.

"For an angel of the Lord descended from heaven and came and rolled back the stone, and sat upon it. His appearance was like lightning, and his raiment white as snow. And for fear of him the guards trembled and became like dead men'' (Mt. 28:2-4).

As they reached the tomb the women were amazed to see that the stone had been rolled away and that an angel sat there. The angel said:

''Do not be afraid; for I know that you seek Jesus who was crucified. He is not here; for he has risen, as he said. Come, see the place where he lay. Then go quickly and tell his disciples that he has risen from the dead'' (Mt. 28:5-7).

The angel represents the spiritual I AM.

''The first affirmation of the I AM for its body is that it is not under any limitation of material thought; that it is free with the freedom of Spirit. 'He is not here; for he has risen.' The second affirmation of the I AM for its body is a swift and universal proclamation of omnipresence and activity in all realms of consciousness. 'Go quickly and tell his disciples that he has risen' '' (MD 349).

In a tumult of rapture and excitement the women hurried back to Jerusalem and told the

Apostles what they had seen and heard. The men were incredulous, but when Mary Magdalene went to Peter and John privately with her news, they ran to the burying place. John outran Peter, but the former did not enter the tomb first. When Peter arrived, he went into the tomb and found the linen cloths and the napkin that had covered the body of Jesus. Then John entered and saw that the tomb was empty. Faith (Peter) is often more courageous than love (John), but both see and believe.

The Apostles and the women seemed to have forgotten Jesus' promise that He would rise from the dead.

"It is not at all surprising that the very near friends of Jesus were filled with astonishment and fear when they found that He was not in the tomb where they had laid Him. They could not understand that for years He had been training His soul to accomplish this very thing. He had spent whole nights in prayer, and through the intensity of His devotions had made union with Divine Mind. This union was so full and so complete that His whole being was flooded with spiritual life, power, and substance and the wisdom to use them in divine order. In this manner He projected the divine-body idea, and through it His mortal body was transformed into an immortal body. This was accomplished before the Crucifixion, and Jesus knew that He had so strengthened His soul that it would restore His body, no matter how harshly the body might be used by destructive man" (MJ 172-173).

Jesus had declared, "I am the resurrection and the life" (Jn. 11:25), and He substantiated this declaration by raising His body. As the Way-Shower, it was necessary for Him to prove that the body can be so transformed that it triumphs over death.

"The resurrection is the lifting up of the whole man into the Christ consciousness. The whole man is spirit, soul, and body. The resurrection lifts up all the faculties of mind until they conform to the absolute ideas of Divine Mind, and this renewal of the mind makes a complete transformation of the body so that every function works in divine order and every cell becomes incorruptible and immortal" (MD 554).

Jesus' promise to each of us is, "He who believes in me, though he die, yet shall he live" (Jn. 11:25). This means that although human-kind, through ignorance, has developed destructive states of mind that are expressed as restricting conditions, we may, through faith in Christ, overcome them and live a new and better life. "And whoever lives and believes in me shall never die" (Jn. 11:26) is the remainder of this promise. This means that those who live in harmony with sprtual laws shall, through continued faith, be able to attain eternal life. The cardinal point of Charles Fillmore's teaching is that each person should bend every effort toward this goal, and He says, "eternal life means continuous conscious existence in the body" (TT 150). It is inevitable that as our consciousness is spiritualized so is our body. We have before us constantly the example of Jesus who, by complete obedience to God, used His body for the right purpose—a temple of the living God. Mr. Fillmore further states:

"Having a body of spiritually electrified atoms, Jesus is able to quicken the bodies of people who attract His presence by believing in Him; He radiates a glorious life that energizes those who believe in His power.

"By positive affirmations we must all appropriate this same Christ life, substance, and Truth as ours individually and as the very foundation and substance of our body.

"Thousands in this day have found the law that Jesus demonstrated and the inner meaning of the Truth that He taught. They are working, praying, denying, affirming, concentrating, willing. They are in all ways building up the perfect-idea body, transforming flesh corruptible into substance incorruptible. Thus they are following Jesus in the regeneration. When they have renewed every organ and every part both within and without, and have put away all evidences of old age, the world at large will begin to accept their claims as true: that the destiny of all men is to transform the body of flesh into a body of Spirit and thus immortalize it. In this manner death is to be overcome and the earth made the dwelling place of immortal men" (MJ 173-174).

Appearances

During the forty days following His resurrection, Jesus appeared to His followers on ten occasions. "Jesus had obtained power on the three planes of consciousness: the spiritual, the psychical, and the material. After His resurrection He held His body on the psychical and the astral planes for forty days'' (MJ 173). His resurrected body was sufficiently similar in appearance to His physical body that He was recognized by many to whom He appeared. His mission was not complete until His followers were convinced of the Resurrection. The eleven Apostles were to continue the Christ ministry, and they had to be convinced that He still lived. But since His body had been spiritualized it was not subject to physical limitations. He could suddenly appear to people in rooms where doors were closed, and could just as suddenly vanish from their sight.

In the years of their association with Jesus, the Apostles had never comprehended His predictions about the Crucifixion and the Resurrection. When He came to them in His resurrected body, they remembered what He had said and at last understood Him. In the garden of Gethsemane, the Apostles had been so confused and fearful that they had deserted Jesus. As a result of His appearances after the Resurrection, the loyalty and faith of the Apostles were renewed and they became the leaders of a faithful and united group.

These appearances are as much a part of Jesus' life as are the three years of His ministry. They verify His claim that spiritual man is all-powerful. Like the disciples of His day, Christians throughout the ages have needed such verification. Some of His richest teaching was given between the Resurrection and the Ascension. While the Gospels give short accounts of a few of His appearances, more than half of them present facts that are vital to a person's spiritual unfoldment. These lend credence to His promise: "I am the light of the world; he who follows me will not walk in darkness, but will have the light of life" (Jn. 8:12).

Five of Jesus' appearances were on the day of the Resurrection (Easter Sunday), and the first of them was to Mary Magdalene.

"Mary stood weeping outside the tomb, and as she wept she stooped to look into the tomb; and she saw two angels in white, sitting where the body of Jesus had lain, one at the head and one at the feet. They said to her, 'Woman, why are you weeping?' She said to them, 'Because they have taken away my Lord, and I do not know where they have laid him' " (Jn. 20:11-13).

Mary's weeping was the human reaction of grief over the death of a loved one, and added to her grief was the fear that someone had stolen Jesus' body. The two angels represent "the positive words of life that bring spiritual powers to bear that lift the body out of matter into Spirit. These two bright and shining powers are possessed of animated intelligence" (MJ 168). Jesus was standing nearby, but Mary's eyes were filled with tears and at first she did not recognize Him. When He asked her why she wept, she thought He was the gardener. However, when He called her by name, she turned, knew Him, and cried: " 'Rabboni!' (which means Teacher). Jesus said to her, 'Do not hold me, for I have not yet ascended to the Father; but go to my brethren and say to them, I am ascending to my Father and your Father, to my God and your God' " (Jn. 20:16-17).

Why did Jesus not want Mary to touch Him? Later in the same afternoon He appeared to other women and did not object if they touched Him. It would seem that Mary was closer to Him than the others, for she had served Him continually from the time He had healed her early in His ministry. Her grief, therefore, was more poignant than theirs. Charles Fillmore gives this explanation:

"The I AM is Spirit, but in order to rise into the realm of pure ideas it must not be attached to the clinging affections of the soul. . . . Jesus did not want the sorrowing Mary thought to touch Him. The spiritual mind does not grieve; it does not look to matter and the limitations of the flesh for life eternal, and it dissipates the thoughts of sorrow by a denial of their reality or power to affect the mind of the Son of God" (MJ 168).

The second appearance of Jesus was to the other women who had come with Mary Magdalene to anoint His body. It probably took place in the garden of Joseph of Arimathaea, and is recorded only in The Gospel According to Matthew.

"And behold, Jesus met them and said, 'Hail!' And they came up and took hold of his feet and worshiped him. Then Jesus said to them, 'Do not be afraid; go and tell my brethren to go to Galilee, and there they will see me'" (Mt. 28:9-10).

As these first appearances were taking place, the guards who had fled from the tomb went to the Jewish authorities and told them of the strange happenings at the tomb. The chief priests and the elders gathered and suggested to these soldiers that they must have fallen asleep and that Jesus' disciples had stolen the body. For a soldier to sleep while on duty was a crime punishable by death, but when the Jewish leaders bribed the soldiers and promised them immunity from punishment to say that Jesus' body had been spirited away, they were glad to spread this report.

Another appearance of Jesus was to Peter. The details of it are unknown, though the visit is referred to by Luke and also by Paul (1 Cor. 15:5). "The Lord has risen indeed, and has appeared to Simon!" (Lk. 24:34)

On the same day toward evening, Jesus appeared to two disciples on the road to Emmaus. This is a beautiful instance of Jesus' desire to open the eyes of those who believe. The two disciples, with sad and anxious hearts, were discussing the incidents of the past two days, when a stranger joined them and asked about their distress. They were surprised that anyone who lived in Jerusalem had not heard of the crucifixion of Jesus of Nazareth, "a prophet mighty in deed and word before God and all the people" (Lk. 24:19). It had been their hope that He was the long-awaited Messiah. True, the report was abroad that He had risen from the dead, but no one had seen Him. These two had not heard of His appearances to Mary Magdalene and the other women. After He reproached the two disciples for their lack of understanding and faith, the Master explained the Old Testament prophecies concerning suffering and glory that were to be experienced by the Savior. When the three arrived at Emmaus, the disciples invited Him to share their food.

"When he was at table with them, he took the bread and blessed, and broke it, and gave it to them. And their eyes were opened and they recognized him; and he vanished out of their sight. They said to each other, 'Did not our hearts burn within us while he talked to us on the road, while he opened to us the scriptures?' " (Lk. 24:30-32)

With all speed the two disciples returned to Jerusalem to tell the great news to the Apostles. They found them and others with them, but before the two could relay their news they were greeted with the joyous tidings, "The Lord is risen indeed." Then the men from Emmaus told of their experience with the risen Savior.

Jesus' fifth appearance was in the evening, and ten of the Apostles (Thomas was not there) were together in a room in Jerusalem. The door was closed. Suddenly:

"Jesus came and stood among them and said to them, 'Peace be with you.' When he had said this, he showed them his hands and his side. Then the disciples were glad when they saw the Lord. Jesus said to them again, 'Peace be with you. As the Father has sent me, even so I send you.' And when he had said this, he breathed on them, and said to them, 'Receive the Holy Spirit. If you forgive the sins of any, they are forgiven; if you retain the sins of any, they are retained' " (Jn. 20:19-23).

John the Baptist had baptized with water unto repentance, but he said of Jesus, "He will baptize you with the Holy Spirit and with fire" (Mt. 3:11).

"The Holy Ghost is the same as the Holy

Spirit or Spirit of truth. When we have received a concept of the relation that we as spiritual beings have to God, the old state of thought is easily dissolved and washed away by that of which water baptism is symbolical—denial. Then there come into our mind ideas direct from the Fountainhead, and we see everything in a new light. This baptism of the Holy Spirit quickens the whole man. When the mind has received words of Truth the way is open for the healing power, which is called the Holy Spirit, or the Spirit of wholeness, to descend further into the body consciousness. This outpouring, or inpouring, of the Holy Spirit is the second baptism'' (MD 96).

This second baptism may be considered as the taking on of divine ideas by affirmation.

The ten Apostles hastily conveyed the glad tidings of Jesus' appearance to Thomas. To him the news seemed too good to be true, and he said:

"Unless I see in his hands the print of the nails, and place my finger in the mark of the nails, and place my hand in his side, I will not believe'' (Jn. 20:25).

A week after the Resurrection, Thomas was given the proof he required, for the Eleven Apostles were together on Sunday evening when Jesus appeared. He invited Thomas to see His hands and feel His side. "Do not be faithless, but believing" (Jn. 20:27). Then Thomas exclaimed, "My Lord and my God!" (Jn. 20:28) and Jesus said:

"Have you believed because you have seen me? Blessed are those who have not seen and yet believe" (Jn. 20:29).

Thomas represents the understanding that, in the natural man, is dubious until it is convinced by proof. Jesus respected the demand of Thomas for physical evidence and gave it to him. Nevertheless, He commended those who believe even before they see the proof. When understanding becomes spiritually quickened it is the perceptive power of the mind and develops in us "the power to use the attributes of God and to understand their place and their work in the Deity. Spiritual understanding enables the consciousness to see and feel spiritually. Spiritual understanding gives clear insight into everything; it remolds the mentality, and inspires the will to direct, to act, and to control'' (CE 62-63).

The day of the seventh appearance of Jesus is not known. It took place early one morning at the Sea of Tiberias (Sea of Galilee), where seven of the Apostles had been fishing all night. Just as day was breaking Jesus appeared on the shore. From a distance, those in the boat did not know that it was He. Calling to them, Jesus asked if they had caught any fish, and when they replied in the negative, He said:

" 'Cast the net on the right side of the boat, and you will find some.' So they cast it, and now they were not able to haul it in, for the quantity of fish'' (Jn. 21:6).

John was the first to recognize Jesus. "It is the Lord!'' he said, and then the impetuous Peter jumped into the sea and swam to shore. There they found prepared a meal of fish and bread, which Jesus invited them to eat.

"Man's mind is the net that catches thoughts, which are the basis of external conditions. The sea is the mental realm in which man exists. . . . The net of man's thought works hard and long in the darkness of human understanding and gains but little, but once the Christ Mind is perceived and obeyed the net is cast on the 'right side,' and success follows. The 'right side' is the side on which man realizes the truth that inexhaustible resources are always present and can be made manifest by those who exercise their faith in that direction. . . .

"The bread and fish that Jesus provided on the shore represents the supply of Spirit for the needs of the body. Not only does the Father provide for man in the natural world, as by the draught of fishes, but in the invisible world of substance are elements that correspond to the material things. Bread symbolizes the substance of the omnipresent Christ body and fish the capacity of increase that goes with it. Fish are the most prolific of all living things and aptly exemplify the ability of increase inherent in the Christ substance" (MJ 177-178).

After the meal Jesus addressed Peter, "Do you love me more than these?" And Peter replied, "Yes, Lord; you know that I love you." Then Jesus said to him, "Feed my lambs" (Jn. 21:15). Three times He asked for an acknowledgment of Peter's love, and three times Peter expressed his love. Three times Jesus commanded Peter to serve humankind. Peter had denied the Lord thrice, and Jesus gave him this opportunity to overcome his vacillating faith by affirming his devotion to Him. True faith has its roots in love for Christ and a willingness to serve Him.

Still addressing Peter, Jesus said:

" 'When you were young, you girded yourself and walked where you would; but when you are old, you will stretch out your hands, and another will gird you and carry you where you do not wish to go.' (This he said to show by what death he was to glorify God.)" (Jn. 21:18-19)

This cryptic prediction is explained by Charles Fillmore:

"Faith (Peter), when it first begins to awaken to the Christ ideal, sees the unlimited possibilities that are presented in this new life; it realizes that it can bring into manifestation anything that may be desired. In its more mature state it realizes the necessity for service in a universal sense. The giving up of the personal self (with the consequent working from a universal standpoint) is the death whereby we are to glorify God. However laying hold of Spirit and its power should accompany the denial of self'' (MJ 179-180).

After Jesus had given this prediction, Peter turned and saw John, who was following them. Peter had received his orders from the Master, and perhaps human curiosity assailed him, for he asked, "Lord, what about this man?" Jesus' reply was a rebuke. "If it is my will that he remain until I come, what is that to you? Follow me!" (Jn. 21:21-22) The highest duty of each of us is to follow Him. We should do our appointed work and not concern ourselves with what another does or fails to do. Our faith faculty (Peter) is inquisitive and dictatorial at times. We should put it under the dominion of the Christ, who alone knows how each faculty should function.

During the meal of the fish and bread Jesus may have told His Apostles about the mountain in Galilee where He would meet all who believed in Him. This was probably Mount Tabor, where more than five hundred assembled at the appointed time. The gospels of Matthew and Mark record this meeting and the words of Jesus at this time. The accounts are different, and each gives a commission to those who love Jesus and are endeavoring to do His will and His work.

(Another commission was given at the last appearance of Jesus before the Ascension and is recorded in The Acts of the Apostles.)

The commission according to Matthew:

"Jesus came and said to them, 'All authority in heaven and on earth has been given to me. Go therefore and make disciples of all nations, baptizing them in the name of the Father and of the Son and of the Holy Spirit, teaching them to observe all that I have commanded you; and lo, I am with you always, to the close of the age' " (Mt. 28:18-20).

Functioning in our spiritual nature, we assert divine authority over all things (heaven and earth). In the consciousness of our Christ self, we are to teach His word, denying and affirming (baptizing) in the threefold nature of the Divine (Father, Son, and Holy Spirit). We can do this only as we are continually aware that we labor in His name and that He is always with us.

The commission according to Mark:

"And he said to them, 'Go into all the world and preach the gospel to the whole creation. He who believes and is baptized will be saved; but he who does not believe will be condemned. And these signs will accompany those who believe: in my name they will cast out demons; they will speak in new tongues; they will pick up serpents, and if they drink any deadly thing, it will not hurt them; they will lay their hands on the sick, and they will recover' '' (Mk. 16:15-18).

The followers of Jesus are to tell the good news of the indwelling Christ to all ("the whole creation"). Those who have ears to hear Truth shall be saved from mortal limitations, while those who close their ears must remain in subjection to the restrictions that result from error thoughts. All who believe and proclaim Truth shall have the dominion and mastery of the spiritual and be able to do the works of Jesus (cast out demons, speak with new tongues, and heal the sick).

The ninth appearance of Jesus is not recorded in The Gospels but is alluded to in Paul's first epistle to the Corinthians: "Then he appeared to James, then to all the apostles" (1 Cor. 15:7).

The last appearance was to the eleven Apostles just before the Ascension.

"And while staying with them he charged

them not to depart from Jerusalem, but to wait for the promise of the Father, which, he said, 'you heard from me, for John baptized with water, but before many days you shall be baptized with the Holy Spirit.' So when they had come together, they asked him, 'Lord, will you at this time restore the kingdom to Israel?' He said to them, 'It is not for you to know times or seasons which the Father has fixed by his own authority. But you shall receive power when the Holy Spirit has come upon you; and you shall be my witnesses in Jerusalem and in all Judea and Samaria and to the end of the earth' '' (Acts 1:4-8).

Here is Jesus' promise of the descent of power from on high to those who are faithful to Him. Only then can we fulfill the provisions of what is sometimes called the great commission, namely, to be His witnesses to people everywhere. ''Unto the end of the earth'' means to serve to the fullest extent in speaking His word, performing His works, and declaring to all the resurrecting power of Christ.

Ascension

Jesus had purposely kept His body on the psychical and astral planes for forty days in order to be with those who were to carry on His work and to complete His instructions to them. At the end of this time He made the final step in the spiritualization of His body, and the Ascension took place.

"And when he had said this, as they were looking on, he was lifted up, and a cloud took him out of their sight. And while they were gazing into heaven as he went, behold, two men stood by them in white robes, and said, 'Men of Galilee, why do you stand looking into heaven? This Jesus, who was taken up from you into heaven, will come in the same way as you saw him go into heaven.' Then they returned to Jerusalem" (Acts 1:9-12).

As regards the Ascension, Charles Fillmore states:

"Through His spiritual attainments Jesus formed a spiritual zone in the earth's mental atmosphere; His followers make connection with that zone when they pray in His 'name.' He stated this fact in John 14:2: 'I go to prepare a place for you.' Simon Peter said, 'Lord, whither goest thou?' Jesus answered him, 'Whither I go, thou canst not follow me now, but thou shalt follow afterwards.'

"When Jesus had purified His body sufficiently, He ascended into this 'place' in the spiritual ethers of our planet. In our high spiritual realizations we make temporary contact with Him and His spiritual character, represented by His 'name.' But we, like the apostles, are not yet able to go there and abide, because we have not overcome earthly attachments. We shall however attain the same freedom and spiritual power that He attained if we follow Him in the regeneration. But we should clearly understand that we cannot go to Jesus' 'place' through death. We must overcome death as He did before we can be glorified with Him in the 'heavens,' the higher realms of the mind" (JC 83-84).

Yet even before we make the final attainment, we may walk in the footsteps of Jesus. This is possible with His loving assistance for which we should ask with all the simplicity and faith of a little child. Truly:

"Jesus still lives in the spiritual ethers of this world and is in constant contact with those who raise their thoughts to Him in prayer. The promise was not an idle one that He would be with those who have faith in Him. 'Let not your heart be troubled, neither let it be fearful. Ye heard how I said to you, I go away, and I come unto you.'

"His body disappeared from our fleshly eyes because He raised it to its true place in the ether; but He can make His presence felt to anyone who looks to Him for help" (JC 11-12).

Each day presents a chance for us to go a little farther along the way that leads to eternal life. Ours is the awe and joy that was in the heart of Andrew when he exclaimed, "We have found the Messiah" (Jn. 1:41). His words ring in the depths of our being, and we are humbly grateful to be able to accept His final commission and tell about the resurrecting power of Spirit that lifts us from the dregs of human misery to the glory of the Christ life. In many quiet meditations we catch the vision that was Paul's, and hear the words that He speaks to each one, "Christ in you, the hope of glory."

INDEX

About the Author

Elizabeth Sand Turner was born on July 5, 1897, in Nashville, Tennessee. Raised as an Episcopalian, she became interested in Unity when her mother, Elizabeth Pierce Sand, visited Unity School in Kansas City in 1910 and received a healing.

Elizabeth Turner's mother founded the Unity center in Nashville in 1916. While Turner attended occasionally, she did not take an active role in the church. She worked with the Nashville, Chattanooga, and St. Louis Railway and, for a time, became business manager and secretary for a lecturer on practical psychology.

A visit by Unity lecturer Francis Gable in 1932 motivated Elizabeth to explore Unity again. In the fall of that year she enrolled in the Unity Correspondence School and became the spiritual leader of the Nashville center in 1933. In 1934 she was licensed a Unity teacher and then ordained as a minister in July 1936.

Elizabeth served as minister at the Unity Center of Christianity in Nashville until 1945. In 1946 she became a field lecturer for Unity School and in the fall of that year was made educational director of the ministerial training school. She worked there until 1955. In 1958 she moved to

Fort Lauderdale, Florida, and served as minister at the Unity church there until August 1966. Elizabeth Sand Turner made her transition on May 1, 1979.

A lover of music and of the Bible, Elizabeth studied the Bible at Peabody College in Nashville. She is now best known for her trilogy of books on the Bible metaphysically interpreted: Let There Be Light (1954), Your Hope of Glory (1959), and Be Ye Transformed (1969). Let There Be Light is dedicated to her mother, Elizabeth Pierce Sand, "who first inspired in me a love for God."

Printed U.S.A.   67-2076-75C-1-96